RECONSIDERING RETIREMENT

RECONSIDERING RETIREMENT

How Losses and Layoffs Affect Older Workers

COURTNEY C. COILE
and
PHILLIP B. LEVINE

BROOKINGS INSTITUTION PRESS
Washington, D.C.

Copyright © 2010
THE BROOKINGS INSTITUTION
1775 Massachusetts Avenue, N.W., Washington, DC 20036
www.brookings.edu

Library of Congress Cataloging-in-Publication data
Coile, Courtney.
   Reconsidering retirement : how losses and layoffs affect older workers / Courtney C.
Coile and Phillip B. Levine.
      p.   cm.
   Includes bibliographical references and index.
   Summary: "Examines effects of the 2008–09 financial downturn on all workers with
particular attention to low-income older workers who stand to suffer the most, often
retiring early because of lack of work; discusses the real effects of the stock market de-
cline, falling house prices, and stagnant job market"—Provided by publisher.
   ISBN 978-0-8157-0499-7 (hardback : alk. paper)
   1. Older people—Employment.   2. Age and employment.   3. Financial crises—
21st century.   I. Levine, Phillip B.   II. Title.
   HD6279.C65 2010
   331.3'980973—dc22   2010030575

9 8 7 6 5 4 3 2 1

Printed on acid-free paper

Typeset in Sabon

Composition by R. Lynn Rivenbark
Macon, Georgia

Printed by R. R. Donnelley
Harrisonburg, Virginia

To our families

HENRY, NATHANIEL, AND MEREDITH

HEIDI, JAKE, AND NOAH

Contents

Acknowledgments

The process of writing and publishing this book was made possible by the important contributions of many individuals, who collectively provided assistance every step of the way. We have the good fortune to have benefited from discussion with and gained insight from several colleagues. At Wellesley, Kristin Butcher and Robin McKnight have been particularly helpful, along with other members of our department who participated in seminars we gave. We have presented our work at a number of other institutions as well—the National Bureau of Economic Research, Brandeis University, Columbia University, Harvard University, the University of Illinois, the Massachusetts Institute of Technology, and the University of Pennsylvania—and we greatly appreciate the comments of those who attended these talks. Although we bear full responsibility for the content of this book, we could not have written it without our peers' contributions.

We are also grateful to a number of individuals at the Brookings Institution for their support and guidance throughout. We first approached Bill Gale with the idea for this book, and his enthusiasm for the project got the ball rolling. Bob Faherty, vice president and director of Brookings Institution Press, immediately committed to the project, encouraged us to complete the manuscript, and oversaw our activities during the writing phase. He also identified two anonymous reviewers who painstakingly read and commented on the original manuscript submission. In particular, they pushed us to elaborate on our policy recommendations; doing so, we believe, made the book much better. The Brookings staff, including Janet Walker and Larry Converse, skillfully guided us through the editorial and production process in bringing the book out into the world.

Others also supported our work in important ways. We are grateful to Samantha Heep and Rebecca Cannon, two of our former students at Wellesley College, for reading the manuscript at a moment's notice when we needed fresh eyes to evaluate what we had written.

Financial support for the project was provided by the Social Security Administration, the W. E. Upjohn Institute for Employment Research, and Wellesley College, and we are indebted to each of these institutions for support. We appreciate the assistance that David Wise, Jeff Brown, and Janet Stein at the NBER provided in supporting our efforts to obtain funding for the project.

And last, but clearly not least, we extend our deepest gratitude to our families and friends, whose moral support helped provide the necessary environment for us to dedicate ourselves to this project.

Prologue

We include this prologue to set the stage for the arguments we make in the chapters that follow. Newspaper stories reprinted here typify much of the press coverage dedicated to the impact of the economic crisis that began in 2008 on workers' retirement plans. At the time these stories appeared, between fall 2008 and fall 2009, the media's predominant assumption was that older workers would be forced to delay retirement because of their falling stock portfolios and, to a lesser extent, slumping house prices. The premise of our book, however, is that media accounts such as these seriously missed the real story: that older workers will be forced to retire early because jobs simply won't exist, and thousands of low-income Americans will face greater economic hardship for the rest of their lives.

This article from the Washington Post *of October 2008 is among the first to claim that older workers will delay retirement because of tumbling stock prices. Although the Navy employee it features is considerably younger than traditional retirement age, the writer highlights the concern that those approaching retirement will be forced to keep their jobs because of stock losses.*

Will You Retire?
New Economic Realities Keep More Americans in the Workforce Longer

Nancy Trejos

Jan Fitzsimmons had the luxury of being able to retire at 47 after 22 years of service with the U.S. Navy.

But retirement turned out to be not so luxurious.

Now 52 and renting an Arlington townhouse, she is looking for part-time work because life has become too expensive. Her grocery bills have gone up. So have her telephone and cable bills. Health insurance, too, is getting costlier.

"Oh yeah, I'm feeling the pinch," she said. "I'm seeing all my investments go down and the cost of living go up."

Many retirees and soon-to-be retirees are reckoning with a new reality: It's just too difficult to live on a fixed income when the price of everything is edging up. At a time when they need more money because of longer life expectancies, many are facing a retirement with less because the wildly fluctuating stock market has depleted 401(k) plans and individual retirement accounts. Meanwhile, more and more employers are moving away from defined benefit plans, such as pensions, in which they guarantee workers a certain amount of money for retirement.

As a result, Americans are increasingly postponing retirement or getting part-time or even full-time work in other fields after retiring.

"Clearly there's a lot of angst around the notion that the economy is making people's 401(k) portfolios be less than what they anticipated, and therefore, the need to postpone retirement is more imminent than before," said Deborah Russell, director of workforce issues at AARP, the nonprofit organization that represents the interests of people 50 and over.

The percentage of older people in the workforce has been rising steadily since the late 1990s after hitting historic lows through the 1980s and early 1990s, according to the U.S. Bureau of Labor Statistics, which is expecting that trend to accelerate. By 2016, the bureau predicts that the number of workers age 65 and over will soar by more than 80 percent, accounting for 6.1 percent of the total labor force. In 2006, they made up just 3.6 percent of active workers.

Older workers are increasingly more comfortable with the notion that traditional retirement might not be in store for them, the AARP has found. According to a survey released by the organization in September, seven in 10 older workers expect to be employed in retirement, mainly part-time. Sixty-four percent of those workers cited current financial needs, such as health care costs, as the primary reason for working, while another 11 percent said future financial security is what's driving them. Another AARP survey released in April showed that 27 percent of older workers had postponed plans to retire because of the economic downturn.

"If we had $2-a-gallon gas and there were no foreclosures and life was good, I think people would probably favor traditional retirement," said Bob Skladany, a human resources consultant and vice president of research and certification for RetirementJobs.com. "I think we've hit a turning point. Expenses won't change. People don't hope to die sooner, so people will work past retirement."

Although many employers are scaling back on hiring because of the anemic economy, others in thriving fields such as health care are recognizing that a brain drain could happen if baby boomers eligible for retirement actually settle into lives on golf courses. Fearful that they wouldn't have enough younger workers to replace them, the prospect of being able to hold on to their trained workforce is appealing, so much so that they don't mind the potentially high health care costs that come with an aging population.

"They're dependable, they're committed, they bring a stabilization to our environment," said R. Virginia Smith, Wal-Mart's senior manager of diversity relations for mature markets. She said the company employs more than 355,000 workers over 50, and even as old as 103, in its stores. The company has about 1.2 million employees. There are now so many retirees expecting to work longer that a new term has been coined for what they are doing: They are "rewiring," not retiring.

Businesses and local governments are actively urging older workers to rewire. Web sites such as RetirementJobs.com have sprung up. The jobs range from the kind that teenagers do in the summer, such as retail, to those requiring advanced skills and education levels. The web site YourEncore.com, for instance, recruits mature workers trained to be engineers, scientists, and product developers.

Many state and local offices for the aging and nonprofit service organizations now hold job fairs for older workers. Operation A.B.L.E. (Ability Based on Long Experience) of Greater Boston organized mature worker career fairs for job seekers 45 and older. Meanwhile, many community colleges, such as Central Florida Community College, offer training programs for older workers.

Recognizing the need to match older workers with employers, AARP created a national employer team of more than two dozen employers who actively court mature workers. Last year, the Internal Revenue Service, the U.S. Small Business Administration Office of Disaster Assistance and the Peace Corps became the first federal agencies to join the team. In August, the organization partnered with RetirementJobs.com to expand its online offerings of job search advice.

Often, Skladany said, older workers are surprised at how the process of finding a job has changed so much in recent years. For one thing, so much is done electronically. Skladany often comes across job seekers who don't even have e-mail accounts, much less know how to use the Internet. He advises them to get a computer with a high-speed Internet connection, learn how to use a search engine such as Google, and get an e-mail address and a cell phone.

"Older workers are stunned by this because they still remember the pen-and-pencil days," he said.

Last month, AARP held its second annual job fair at its convention in the District to guide older workers through the process. Organizers said attendance by both job seekers and employers was much higher than last year.

In the middle of the sprawling Washington Convention Center floor were tables with computers where soon-to-be retirees and retirees were looking up job postings in AARP's database. On a nearby stage, consultants gave tips on putting together a résumé and mastering interviews. To the left and right of the stage were booths where potential employers such as Wal-Mart and the IRS were handing out information and interviewing job candidates.

Many of the job seekers were retired and looking for ways to make extra cash. Others had not yet retired but had been laid off or lost contract work due to the weak economy.

Cynthia Thompson-Scott, of Hyattsville, had a contract as an office manager at a private school, but it was not renewed because of downsizing. "I'm 50 years old and I have to look for another job," she said while sitting at a computer. "It's the pits."

Others were simply bored with the slower pace of retirement and eager to find part-time work to keep them occupied. "Retirement for boomers is not the retirement of our grandparents, who played golf," Russell said. "Boomers want to stay engaged, live in metro areas, interact with different generations."

Mary McLean, a 66-year-old Northeast resident, retired earlier this year from her job in the accounting department of Ocean Conservancy, an environmental group.

"I've been home for about six months. I've straightened out the house. I go to the gym every day, so I just needed something to do," she said.

She also wouldn't mind having more spending money. "I have to watch my spending more," she said. "Just going to the gym every day, I have to buy a lot more gas for the car."

Fitzsimmons, the Arlington resident, is not only watching her spending. She's cutting back.

Although she retired from the Navy in 2003, she continued to work on a contract in the defense industry. She gave that up in January and has since been living off her military pension, which amounts to about half of what she earned while working. She has an IRA, mutual funds, money market accounts and a certificate of deposit as her backup.

The lack of extra income from the contract has been noticeable, especially in recent weeks as the economy has deteriorated. She has suspended shopping. She hardly dines out. Her car could use new tires, but she's holding off for now. She recently bundled her phone and cable service to shave off a few dollars from the monthly tab.

"I didn't notice those things as much as I do now that I don't have an extra paycheck," she said. "I'm nervous. I'm very, very nervous."

This next piece, released more than two months later than the Trejos article, on January 31, 2009, introduces the concept that falling home prices may also contribute to delayed retirement.

When Retirement Plans Change
Relying on Home Equity Is No Longer an Option for Many

Adrian Sainz

Many Americans have found themselves changing their plans for retirement after losing a substantial amount of home equity as the housing market and the overall U.S. economy struggle.

Homeowners who have tapped their home equity, then spent it like Monopoly money, find themselves with no more funds to extract.

Ideas of a comfy retirement full of relaxation and travel have been abandoned.

The good news is about 30 percent of homeowners have no mortgage at all. So even though their properties are probably worth less now than a few years ago, these people can tap into that equity cushion if necessary.

The bad news, though, is that about one in six with a mortgage now owe the bank more than their homes are worth, according to Moody's Economy.com. Most are property owners who purchased their homes within the past few years, or refinanced their properties and siphoned off too much equity.

Knowing that, it's time for Americans to explore options other than relying on home equity, especially if they have no other retirement investments or savings. Options include downsizing their home, selling assets, postponing retirement by working longer, and signing up for a reverse mortgage. Each has its challenges and risks.

Ken King, 61, once planned to retire in his early to mid-60s. The value of his home has dropped $70,000, so he's scrapped plans to sell the five-bedroom house and downsize, because the savings won't be substantial enough to make it a smart move. He's also seen his 401(k) lose value.

So, King, a credit counselor in Sheboygan, Wis., says he will likely work into his early 70s to compensate.

"This is something I wouldn't have considered even thinking about 1 1/2 years ago," said King, adding that priorities also have changed this year among those he counsels.

"A year ago, we were talking to people about what they need to do just to make it," King said. "Now we're talking to people about what they have to do to survive."

King's strategy of working longer is increasingly popular. AARP reported in April that almost one in four people from age 45 to 54 planned to delay retirement, with one in five ages 55 to 64 thinking the same.

Staying on the job has benefits besides a paycheck. Employment is often a requisite in qualifying for mortgage refinancing, a good option for those with equity and good credit because rates have fallen to historic lows. But refinancing becomes almost impossible for seniors on fixed incomes with no job or equity.

The scenario becomes more serious if someone has retired and wants to return to the work force, especially as health issues crop up and competition for jobs increases, said George Moschis, director of the Center for Mature Consumer Studies at Georgia State University.

By working later in life, pre-retirees also can consider putting off collecting Social Security, a strategy that could lead to higher monthly payouts once they do start collecting.

Finding a smaller and less expensive home has long been relied upon to bolster retirement budgets. Ideally, profits from the sale of a larger home can be used to buy the smaller home with cash, with no mortgage, and the homeowner can pocket the rest. But the current environment of falling home values and tight credit has made home buying and selling a more difficult proposition in many markets.

Another way to shore up retirement accounts is selling off assets, including cars, second homes, stocks and expensive jewelry. They often have emotional attachments that don't match their resale values.

A reverse mortgage is another option marketed as a way to free up retirement cash.

A reverse mortgage allows homeowners to borrow from the home's equity in a lump sum, line of credit or regular payments, while not having to pay a monthly mortgage. The homeowner retains the title and must pay insurance and property taxes while living there.

The loan and fees are due once all parties listed on the deed die, or the home is vacated for 12 straight months. The home is usually sold, and the proceeds from the sale are used to pay off the loan, plus interest and fees that can be up to 4 to 8 percent of the loan.

Reverse mortgages have become more attractive because the government raised lending limits to $417,000 last year, noted Eric Bachman, chief executive of Golden Gateway Financial in Oakland, Calif. But as equity drops, so does the amount one can borrow in a reverse mortgage, so timing is key.

However, experts such as AARP financial "ambassador" Jonathan Pond say reverse mortgages should be something of a last resort, because of high fees and the complicated nature of the loans. Reverse mortgages also mean the home will probably be sold at the end of the loan, mainly because the homeowner, or an heir, will want cash to pay off the mortgage. Seniors who want to leave their home to their children may not want a reverse mortgage.

The stock market hit bottom in March 2009, about the time this story ran in the Christian Science Monitor. *The press is still focusing on delayed retirement that may result from falling stock and home prices, despite an unemployment rate that had been skyrocketing for six months.*

Economic Crisis Scrambles Retirement Math
The 401(k) Model of Saving Is under Duress as Stocks Slide. Home Equity Losses Don't Help.

Mark Trumbull

The recession has pushed retirement further out on the horizon for millions of Americans—and is putting severe strain on the 401(k) model of retirement saving.

If that wasn't already clear, a bout of stock market selling early this week brought the challenge into sharp relief, as the Standard & Poor's 500 index closed at a level not seen since 1996, down more than 50 percent in 17 months. Coupled with huge losses of home equity in the housing market, the result is a historic decline in net worth for US households.

The downturn on Wall Street is still far from matching the nearly 90 percent drop seen in the Great Depression. Many investors are hoping portfolio values will get an upward bounce later this year, if markets begin to focus on recovery rather than risk.

But the setbacks faced by retirees and by workers trying to build nest eggs could have lasting impacts. These may include new policies designed to make retirement funds less exposed to market volatility in the future. At the very least, families are having to save more and to do damage control on retirement plans that have sunk in value.

"The hit is very significant," says Rick Miller, who runs a financial planning consulting firm in Cambridge, Mass. "I'm encouraging people to try to stay on an even keel. And to make decisions that are appropriate to their circumstances."

That may mean sticking with volatile investments, but not in every case.

"I'm not saying to everyone, 'Hang in there with stocks,' because for some clients it may not be the right the decision," Mr. Miller says.

HOUSE HEARINGS

Just last week, the House Committee on Education and Labor held a hearing to consider the challenge of retirement security, in light of the financial crisis.

Alicia Munnell, director of the Center for Retirement Research at Boston College, testified that Americans were poorly prepared for retirement even before the recession began.

"But I thought the dimensions of the problem would not become clear for another 10 or 15 years, when large numbers of people retired reliant solely on Social Security and 401(k)s," she said in her prepared statement. "Instead, the financial crisis has accelerated a reexamination of our retirement income system."

According to the center's research, 44 percent of Americans in 2006 were "at risk" of having insufficient income for retirement. When broken into three income groupings and three age groupings, Americans' vulnerability levels ranged from 28 percent, for one group of early baby boomers, to 60 percent—that's the share of low-income Generation Xers who were at risk.

Now, the recession and the related loss of wealth are pushing those risk percentages upward. In one sense, the setback for the typical household is smaller than the bear market in stocks implies. Many Americans have no retirement account, and those who have work-based accounts don't put all their savings in stocks.

SAVERS LOSE 25 TO 30 PERCENT

Since January 2008, people who have been saving in a workplace plan for a period of 10 to 19 years have seen their account balances fall, on average, by 25 to 30 percent, much less than the S&P index during that time, according to numbers gathered by the Employee Benefit Research Institute in Washington.

But for many families, the home itself is the largest asset, one that may have declined a lot in value, depending on where they live.

"Millions of middle-class homeowners still have little or no equity even after they have been homeowners for several decades," write economists Dean Baker and David Rosnick, of the Center for Economic and Policy Research, in a new report on baby boomers and the housing collapse.

COPING STRATEGIES

Americans are already beginning to adapt by working longer, saving more, and in some cases rethinking how exposed they want to be to the stock market.

Most Americans haven't lost all appetite for investing in stocks, as occurred for a generation following the market crash that began in 1929. But some people with low risk tolerance are getting out of stocks for good, Miller says.

At the least, the bear market—worse than any since the Depression—serves as a reminder that stocks can go down even if you hold for a decade or more.

"I do believe it's true that stocks have higher returns" than other investments, in general, Miller says. But "a lot of people had the view that was a sure thing."

Whether people stay in stocks or not, what's vital is to have contingency plans, such as fixed-income investments, in case stocks do badly, he says.

Alan Lancz, an asset manager in Toledo, Ohio, says he's been putting more client money into bonds over the past 18 months, even as he sees a buying opportunity for stocks if share prices dip further.

Financial publications nowadays are matching investment tips with advice on how to spend less, such as a "101 ways to cut expenses" article on the investment website Morningstar.

AMERICANS SAVING 5 PERCENT

America's savings rate, as measured by the Commerce Department, rose to 5 percent of income in the most recent quarter. Many economists expect that number to go higher still.

And workers are postponing retirement. According to a new survey sponsored by the investment firm ING Direct, 4 in 10 Americans believe the current economic climate will force them to retire as many as 10 years later than originally expected or not at all.

Some retirement experts call for new savings vehicles that do better at guaranteeing a modest but reliable stream of income. Ideas such as that were among those raised at last week's congressional hearing.

A full year into the crisis, the argument takes a new turn in this article from the New York Times *in September 2009. One of the reasons that unemployed workers cannot find jobs, the article claims, is that workers who would have retired are hanging onto their jobs, clogging the pipeline.*

A Reluctance to Retire Means Fewer Openings

Catherine Rampell and Matthew Saltmarsh

To the long list of reasons American companies aren't hiring—business losses, tight credit, consumer retrenchment—add the fact that many of their older workers are unable, or afraid, to retire.

In other parts of the developed world, people are retiring as planned, because of relatively flush state and corporate pensions that await them. But here in the United States, financial security in old age rests increasingly on private savings, which have taken a beating in the last year.

Prospective retirees are clinging to their jobs despite some cherished life plans.

As a result, companies are not only reluctant to create new jobs, but have fewer job openings to fill from attrition. For the 14 million Americans looking for work—a number expected to rise in Friday's jobs report for August—this lack of turnover has made a tough job market even tougher.

Consider Barbara Petrucci, a dialysis nurse who had expected to stop working soon, or at least scale back to part time. Now that her family savings have been depleted by market declines, she expects to stay on the job for a long, long time.

"Retirement is kind of an elusive dream at this point," says Ms. Petrucci, 58, who works at an Atlanta hospital while her retired husband, Ned, 61, interviews for jobs (unsuccessfully, so far). "We tease at work about someday having to go around at the hospital with our walkers."

The diverted life plans of families like the Petruccis are an unintended economic consequence of the nation's sprawling 401(k) plans. These private retirement savings vehicles, designed 30 years ago as a supplement to traditional corporate pensions, have somewhat haphazardly replaced the old system, like an innocuous weed that somehow overgrew the garden.

As is apparent in this downturn, the economic effects of such an ad hoc system can be perverse. In boom times, when companies need more workers, the most experienced employees may decide to retire, taking comfort in their bloated 401(k)s, whose values typically fluctuate with the financial markets.

Today, the reverse is happening in the first deep recession since the new accounts became so pervasive. A Pew Research survey scheduled for Thursday release found that nearly four in 10 workers over age 62 say they have delayed their retirement because of the recession. (Though the data omit some people who have retired and include some who are still working, the Social Security Administration said that about 2.3 million people that age started collecting benefits last year.)

"One unappreciated side effect of the 401(k) system is that it's a sort of reverse automatic stabilizer," says Teresa Ghilarducci, an economics professor at the New School. The recent retirement losses have prompted policy makers to discuss whether Americans need a stronger social safety net, not just in health care and unemployment benefits, but in retirement as well.

Economists say there are advantages to reducing the financial risk for individuals. Pooling investments, in some cases, allows workers to switch jobs more easily and helps lower fees associated with investment decisions, for example.

Alternatives include creating incentives for saving and for less risky investments through tax laws or other regulations. The Obama administration has proposed an opt-out retirement savings system, for example. And even before the crisis, some states developed plans for pooling private savings into voluntary, portable retirement accounts.

Though their pension systems may be strained, people in many countries with stronger safety nets are still exiting the labor force in lockstep despite the global recession. Last year in the United States, almost a third of people ages 65 to 69 were still in the labor force; in France, just 4 percent of people this age were still working or looking for work.

After all, Europe isn't just the land of "socialized" medicine. It is also the land of "socialized" retirement plans, and like other automatic stabilizers, pensions help cushion the blow of an economic crisis.

Retirement income typically comes from a combination of three buckets: state pensions, corporate pensions and individual arrangements. In many other industrialized countries, that first bucket—state pensions—supports a large amount of retirees' income.

The typical American receives just 45 percent of his preretirement wage through Social Security, according to the Organization for Economic Cooperation and Development. By contrast, a worker in Denmark, which has one of the most comprehensive and generous retirement arrangements in the world, can retire with a state pension that is 91 percent of his salary.

"The financial crisis hasn't affected me," says Jens Erik Soerensen, a 63-year-old in Hellerup, Denmark, who works as a researcher at Chempilots, a Danish company that develops polymers for use in the medical device industry.

Mr. Soerensen has calculated that when he retires, the combined disposable income that he has with his wife (Lone, also 63, who retired this year from her job in TV production) will fall by about 20 percent. The couple will also continue to benefit from universal health coverage.

"I think we can survive without changing our lifestyle, at least until 75," he said. After that, he might have to dip into personal savings.

Of course, such a system comes with tradeoffs. To help pay for generous state pensions, Danish workers have one of the highest tax burdens. The population is also aging, meaning that there will be fewer working people to pay for the pensions and care of a graying society.

In response, some nations have been trying to encourage people to stay at work longer. In France, suggestions to raise the retirement age above its current level of 60 have met fierce opposition from unions, although the government intends to push ahead. Britain has had a bit more success, announcing plans to raise the retirement age to 68, from 65—in 2044.

Along with raising the retirement age, some European countries have been shifting more financial risk to individuals.

In the United States, where the practice is decades old, the question is whether people can be freed from making their own financial decisions, an act they may not feel qualified to do and may not want to do.

One study found that nearly a quarter of Americans ages 56 to 64 had more than 90 percent of their 401(k) balances invested in stocks instead of bonds, against financial advisers' standard advice for people nearing retirement age.

"Employees are just not capable of making these decisions," said Rick K. Shapiro, a member of the army of financial planning professionals that America's private retirement system (and private health care and college education financing systems) has spawned. "Maybe they can learn, but they're distracted, and they're not incented to learn until the thing blows up."

Even conscientious investors—like the Petruccis, who keep an updated spreadsheet of their investments—lose money.

"We thought we were conservative," said Mr. Petrucci, noting that he and his wife lost about 35 percent of their life savings in the crisis and have made only a little of it back.

Still, the American preference for self-reliance, instead of more socialized financial protections, remains strong, even among those who lost big.

"I don't want to depend on anybody else in my retirement," Mr. Petrucci said. "Not family members, not our children, and certainly not the government, for that matter."

The notion that older workers would never be able to retire even made it into the cartoons.

RECONSIDERING RETIREMENT

1 | *Introduction*

The current economic crisis is arguably the most severe the United States has experienced since the Great Depression. Economic activity began falling in the first quarter of 2008 and, with the exception of slow growth in a single quarter in that year, continued to contract through the second quarter of 2009. The unemployment rate surpassed 10 percent in October 2009, having risen more than 5 points since late 2007. These sobering statistics suggest that of the eleven recessions since World War II, this crisis is certainly among the worst. In its wake, millions of Americans have experienced significant economic disruption of their daily lives.

Of the many repercussions of the current crisis, the effects on older workers and their retirement plans have received considerable attention. The steep drop in the stock market decimated 401(k)s and other retirement savings accounts, reducing expected income in retirement. With the collapse of the housing market, older workers have seen their home values plummet as well, further reducing their potential retirement income. The growing unease regarding well-being in retirement, the thinking goes, will prevent people from retiring.

The newspaper articles quoted in the prologue are but a few of the many that have made these points since the crisis began. These articles typically identify individuals—in the ones here, a career naval officer, a credit counselor, and a dialysis nurse—who feel that they may need to keep their jobs even though they had been planning to retire. Falling home prices and lost retirement savings are the culprits. These individuals had been planning a comfortable retirement drawing down funds from a sizable 401(k) account or using the proceeds from downsizing their homes but scrapped these plans when the stock and housing markets crumbled. Now they will continue working.

Television and radio coverage has struck a similar chord. In the spring of 2009, CBS aired "Retirement Dreams Disappear with 401(k)s" on *60 Minutes,* and National Public Radio presented a week-long series entitled "Rethinking Retirement" on *All Things Considered.*[1] News magazines have joined in as well. A *Business Week* cover story, also entitled "Rethinking Retirement," focused on workers' growing concerns about funding their retirement, while *The Economist* suggested "Smaller Nest Eggs Enhance a Long-Term Trend to Later Retirement."[2] Such concerns are far from new, of course. Similar stories surfaced in all the media outlets after the "dot.com" bubble burst and the stock market crashed in the early 2000s, as in *Time* magazine's cover story "Will You Ever Be Able to Retire?" of July 2002.

Recent public opinion polls also seem to suggest that workers will now be delaying retirement. In a Roper survey conducted during the 2008 election season, 53 percent of likely voters felt that the current financial crisis would require them to work longer (GFK Roper Public Affairs and Media, 2008). Pew Research has found almost two-thirds of workers between the ages of fifty and sixty-one expressing the same sentiment (Taylor and others, 2009).

Despite the various reports of public concern, evidence that the economic crisis will delay retirement is far from clear. The number of indi-

---

1. See www.cbsnews.com/stories/2009/04/17/60minutes/main4951968.shtml and www.npr.org/templates/story/story.php?storyId=104355193 (September 8, 2009). The similar title of our book had been selected before the airing of this story.

2. The *Business Week* article ran on July 2, 2009, and *The Economist*'s on September 10, 2009.

viduals filing Social Security retirement claims in the spring of 2009 was considerably higher than the figure for 2008, according to the Social Security Administration (SSA).[3] An update later that year confirmed this point: between 2008 and 2009, the number of workers claiming Social Security retirement benefits rose by 23 percent, well beyond the increase expected simply because of the greater numbers of baby boomers.[4] Both times this information appeared in the press, it received one-day coverage and was quickly replaced by more stories like those in the prologue.

The rising number of Social Security claims suggests there may be more going on here than the media are reporting. If retirements are indeed increasing rather than decreasing in the midst of the worst economic crisis in decades, what could explain this trend? One hint comes from the news coverage itself. For the dialysis nurse in the *New York Times* article, another factor pushing her to delay retirement is that her sixty-one-year-old husband is unable to find work. If his poor luck continues, he may end up claiming Social Security benefits when he hits age sixty-two, providing income support for the family but withdrawing from the labor force at the same time. The weak labor market may force him and other workers like him into early retirement.

In other words, it is difficult to know what impact the current economic crisis may have on retirement behavior. Decreases in retirement savings account balances and home equity reduce available income in retirement and may indeed lead some to stay in the workforce longer. At the same time, a weak labor market may lead to job losses and limit opportunities for older workers who are seeking jobs. Their only option may be to retire. Both delayed retirement for some and earlier retirement for others may result.

3. For an example of the stories covering this announcement, see Mike Dorning, "Early Retirement Claims Increase Dramatically," *Los Angeles Times*, May 24, 2009.

4. Stephen Ohlenmacher, "Job Losses, Early Retirements Hurt Social Security" (http://abcnews.go.com/Politics/wireStory?id=8683983).

Perhaps more important, different socioeconomic groups may respond differently to the crisis. Those who choose to work longer because of lost retirement savings or home equity would need to have had substantial holdings to be affected in any meaningful way; more highly educated workers are more likely to be in this position. On the other hand, those unable to find work are likely to be in the less-skilled group, as it tends to struggle the most when the labor market is weak.

Our interest in the effects of the economic crisis on retirement is motivated not only by an interest in retirement itself but also by a broader concern about the well-being of older individuals. In nonmonetary respects, working can provide individuals with a sense of purpose, a place to go in the morning, a means to connect with co-workers who may also be friends, and the like. Retirement may be difficult because of the loss of these things. On the other hand, retirement may also mean the end of dealing with a difficult boss, physical pain from the strain of the work, or mental anguish from the pressure to perform. Hence retirement can be associated with positive or negative changes in a worker's well-being.

But the main reason that most individuals work is to put food on the table, pay the mortgage, and cover the car payments, so the most important implications of retirement are those for the worker's financial well-being. As long as the individual keeps working, the flow of labor earnings keeps coming. Once the worker retires, consumption has to be financed out of whatever resources have been accumulated up to that point.

For most older individuals, the main sources of income in retirement are Social Security, private pensions, and savings. The earlier a worker taps into these resources, the smaller his or her income will be. Social Security benefits are available starting at age sixty-two, and the amount depends on the age at which benefits are claimed. The sooner benefits begin, the smaller the monthly check will be, and it will remain the same (not counting inflation adjustments) for the rest of the claimant's life. Private pensions paid out monthly work in much the same way. For any account-based pension or private savings, retiring earlier will mean a longer period of retirement to finance, so there will necessarily be less money available from these sources in any given year.

If workers retire earlier or later than expected in response to the economic crisis, this may have important implications for their well-being far beyond the initial retirement decision. A worker who is laid off, unable to find new work, and forced to start collecting Social Security benefits to make ends meet now will find those benefits permanently reduced. A worker who loses a large portion of a 401(k) fund or other investments and chooses to work a few more years to conserve assets and replace some of the lost savings may contain the damage to that short period of time if retirement is delayed sufficiently. If not, less money will be available throughout retirement.

The implications of the crisis for retiree well-being, as for retirement, may vary with the type of worker. Less-skilled older workers, who are most likely to be affected by the weak labor market, may have fewer resources other than Social Security to provide income during retirement. For them, the decrease in the monthly benefit amount resulting from claiming early may represent a sizable reduction in their total retirement income. More-skilled, higher-earning older workers may experience meaningful losses of retirement income when the stock market falls. But, these workers tend to have more stable jobs and may have the option to work a few extra years to help make up for their losses. Even if they are unable to continue working, their lost retirement income may be a smaller share of their total income and thus be easier to absorb. The impact of the crisis on their well-being in retirement may be much smaller than it is for the less-skilled workers.

Given that the depth of the current crisis motivates our analysis, does this suggest that our findings will become less relevant as the economy improves? The answer is clearly no.

First, as of this writing, the economic recovery still has a long way to go. While the stock market is up significantly from its low in the spring of 2009, it has thus far only made up about half of the losses incurred over the previous eighteen months. Moreover, the labor market remains very weak. The unemployment rate is still close to 10 percent, up more than 5 points from its 2007 value, and has declined only very slightly since the peak of the crisis. It is likely to take many years for the economy to add enough jobs to bring the unemployment rate down substantially.

Second, as already discussed, economic crises may have long-term effects on well-being. Even as market conditions improve, the negative consequences of the bust may persist, so it continues to be important to understand these effects. Most important, even with a period of expansion in the labor market and a bull market on Wall Street, the next recession and bear market can only be so far away. It is the nature of markets to cycle up and down. Lessons learned from the current boom-and-bust cycle may help older workers and policymakers to prepare for the next downturn and avoid the worst of its effects.

So far we have put forth a number of hypotheses regarding the impact of the current economic crisis on retirement patterns and the well-being of retirees:

—Falling stock and home prices may lead some older workers to delay retirement.

—Weak labor markets may lead some older workers to retire sooner than expected.

—Retirement responses may differ for more- and less-skilled workers.

—Weak stock, housing, and labor markets may have long-lasting effects on retirement income.

—The crisis may do more harm to the well-being of less-skilled or lower-income retirees.

Only the first point has received significant attention from the public. To the best of our knowledge, there is relatively little empirical evidence to strongly support this proposition. And in spite of all the interest in how the current economic crisis will affect retirement, the remaining hypotheses have by and large gone unnoticed, both by academics studying retirement and by the public at large.

The purpose of this book is to address these issues. How will the current economic crisis affect older workers' decisions to retire? Will they be less likely to retire now that their retirement savings have been depleted? Will their falling home prices similarly encourage them to delay retirement? Or will they find themselves without work and any alternative other than to retire? How will the effects differ for rich and poor workers? How will all of this affect these workers' well-being in retirement?

When we explore these questions, we find support for many of our hypotheses. Much of our analysis concentrates on the retirement decision, separately examining the impact of stock, housing, and labor markets on the transition into retirement. We find evidence indicating that a declining stock market will lead certain workers to delay retirement: namely, the more-skilled ones who are responding to long-term fluctuations in stock prices. Furthermore, weak labor markets appear to increase the likelihood that an individual will withdraw from the labor force earlier, particularly starting at age sixty-two, when Social Security benefits become available. This is primarily the case for less-skilled workers. There is little evidence to indicate that falling home prices matter. Individuals do not seem to alter their retirement behavior in a meaningful way when home prices fall.

We conclude that the current economic crisis will lead both more workers to retire because the labor market is weak and fewer workers to retire because the stock market is weak: according to our estimates, 378,000 workers will be forced to retire because of the weak job market, and 258,000 workers will choose to delay retirement because of the weak stock market. In other words, the increase in retirements associated with higher unemployment is almost 50 percent greater than the decrease (or delay) in retirements associated with lower stock prices. The fact that the two groups of affected workers are very different—those retiring early tend to be less skilled and those retiring late tend to be more skilled—only serves to emphasize the significance of these findings.

Turning to the impact of these decisions on retirees' economic well-being, we find that weak labor markets have important effects here as well. Workers who experienced high unemployment around the time of retirement have lower incomes a decade or so later, largely because of reduced Social Security income. The magnitude of the effect is roughly consistent with the benefit reduction a Social Security recipient would face if claiming benefits at age sixty-two rather than sixty-five. This effect is strongest among lower-income individuals, who have little income beyond Social Security, and represents a substantial income loss for them. Higher-income retirees who experience poor stock market returns around the time of retirement are less likely to receive investment income in retirement or may receive lower levels of investment income. However, these losses represent a relatively small share of their total income.

Taken as a whole, then, retirement problems related to a weak labor market appear to exceed those associated with falling stock prices. Workers affected by weak labor markets are more numerous than those affected by poor stock market returns, are more likely to have low socioeconomic status, and have a more substantially reduced income for the rest of their lives. The public needs to focus considerably more attention on the needs of older workers in lower socioeconomic groups who potentially face years of lower income if a recession occurs near the time of retirement. Though also likely to suffer, the smaller number of workers in higher socioeconomic groups who delay retirement in response to declining stock prices and receive less investment income in retirement will be of somewhat less concern.

Our conclusions emerge from a comprehensive empirical analysis that relies on appropriate statistical tools and the best available data on the employment patterns and income receipt of older individuals. Drawing on large-scale national databases, we use three decades of relevant information on hundreds of thousands of older individuals to examine the impact of changing conditions over time in stock, housing, and labor markets. Data on location of residence are of additional value in that labor market and housing market conditions differ by geography. We also use this variation to shed light on the impact of market conditions on retirement and retiree well-being.

If weak labor markets lead workers to retire earlier and have a negative impact on their subsequent well-being in retirement, what policies might help to alleviate these problems for older workers? First, we support extending unemployment insurance (UI) benefits to age sixty-two during recessions for those workers who lose their jobs at or after age fifty-eight. Many laid-off older workers struggle to find adequate sources of income support until they become eligible for Social Security benefits; these workers are, in essence, crawling across the finish line. The extension of UI until age sixty-two during recessions would provide a needed bridge to Social Security.

Second, we endorse changing the calculation of Social Security benefits for older individuals to include a credit for a period of late-career unemployment. As we explain in more detail in chapter 8, doing so would provide a modest boost to workers' monthly Social Security benefits, thereby improving their financial well-being for the rest of their lives.

Third, we recommend communicating to workers the option of stopping and starting their Social Security benefits. This policy would encourage laid-off older workers to keep looking for work even at or after age sixty-two and thus reduce the financial consequences of a late-career layoff for those who ultimately found work. The cost of all of these policies would be relatively modest, and the risk that they would induce workers to voluntarily become or stay unemployed would be acceptably low.

We present some baseline facts in chapter 2, in preparation for the more sophisticated statistical results that follow. These facts relate to questions of interest in the book. How have retirement patterns been changing over time? How do retirement patterns typically change year by year as workers age? What are the sources of income received by retirees, and how do the amounts differ by socioeconomic status? What aspects of Social Security and pension rules are important for retirement decisions and retiree well-being?

Further details regarding the data and our specific methods of analysis are presented in chapter 3. Briefly, we compare retirement behavior and subsequent retiree well-being for workers who approach retirement age in similar circumstances but face different market conditions. For instance, we explore whether workers in their early sixties who live in areas or periods of high unemployment retire earlier than others of the same age who live at a time and in a place where the labor market is strong.

Chapters 4, 5, and 6 present the core of our analysis regarding the impact of fluctuating market conditions on retirement behavior. These chapters focus on the stock, housing, and labor markets, respectively, but the data and methods used in each are very similar.

In chapter 7, we explore the impact of market conditions on retiree well-being after retirement, focusing on the role of stock and labor markets. We omit the housing market because we are unable to find any evidence of an impact of this market on retirement decisions in chapter 5.

We review our findings in chapter 8 and discuss their policy implications. This discussion makes clear that the public has been somewhat misguided in its extensive attention to the impact of declining stock prices on retirement. Public policy needs to focus more on the role that skyrocketing unemployment will play in determining retirement behavior and subsequent well-being.

2 | *Defining and Explaining* Retirement

What are the relevant trends in retirement behavior? What do researchers already know about how workers make retirement decisions? And what is retirement, anyway? We explore these fundamental questions in this chapter as background for our subsequent analysis.

What Is "Retirement"?

Any analyst who wishes to study retirement behavior must first decide on a definition of retirement. It turns out that this is no easy task. Merriam-Webster's Dictionary defines retirement as "withdrawal from one's position or occupation or from active working life," which suggests that retirement may be a state of mind as much as anything else. The analyst, however, needs a more concrete definition, and there are many possibilities for this.

Defined in terms of labor force participation, retirement would be the moment at which an individual stops working for pay. Another definition might focus on departure from a full-time "career job" held for many years, even if the worker went on to hold a part-time or less-intense job for some years thereafter. Still another definition might relate to the initial claim of Social Security benefits, an important milestone for retirees. In addition, retirement status might be defined on the basis of self-reports, as recorded in some surveys.

Not surprisingly, then, an individual's status can vary, depending on the definition of retirement used. Consider a worker who leaves his career job at age sixty, works part-time at a new job until age sixty-five, claims Social Security benefits at age sixty-two, and does unpaid volunteer work until age seventy, at which point he finally considers himself retired. This worker might be classified as having retired at any of those ages, depending on the retirement definition used.

Two labor force patterns that are not infrequent among older workers can further muddy the waters. The first is the use of so-called bridge jobs after workers leave their full-time career jobs and before they fully withdraw from the labor force. Recent research (Cahill, Giandrea, and Quinn, 2005) suggests that one-half to two-thirds of workers with full-time career jobs turn to a bridge job before exiting the labor force.

The second pattern is labor force reentry, or a return to work after some period of not working. This is much less common than the use of bridge jobs but nonetheless raises a quandary for the researcher.[1] If a worker exits the labor force after a particular age, say, age fifty-five, and subsequently reenters it at a later date, when can he or she be said to have retired—after the first exit or the second?

In the end, our approach to defining retirement is driven by the data at our disposal rather than by any particular philosophical view of retirement. As discussed in chapter 3, we draw those data from the Current Population Survey (CPS) for March of each year, which dictates that we define retirement as complete withdrawal from the labor force, rather than as a departure from a career job or a self-report of being retired. Since the CPS does not follow the same workers long enough for

1. Studies by Bruce, Holtz-Eakin, and Quinn (2000) and Coile and Levine (2006) suggest that the average rate of reentry for older workers is on the order of 2 to 4 percent a year. Maestas (2007) reports higher rates of what she terms "unretirement," with 26 percent of workers unretiring over a six-year period. However, her definition of unretirement is somewhat broader than our definition of labor force reentry, including, for example, transitions from part-time work to full-time work.

us to observe all possible future labor force reentry, we treat any labor force exit starting at age fifty-five as a retirement. In defining retirement in this way, we are following much of the previous literature.

Trends and Patterns in Retirement Behavior

Over the past several decades, economists have conducted a tremendous amount of research on retirement. Why this great interest? One important factor has been a desire to explain some striking changes in the labor force behavior of older workers in the United States since World War II.

These changes are evident in the labor force participation rate, which is the share of the population that is either working or looking for work. In the period 1948–2008, the rate for men aged fifty-five to sixty-four fell dramatically, from 90 percent in 1948 to 66 percent in 1994. The decline was particularly steep in the 1970s, when participation fell by more than 10 percentage points. From the mid-1980s to the mid-1990s, male participation was essentially flat, but it has begun to climb since then and is now up 5 points from its lowest value.

While statistics on the average retirement age are harder to come by, the decrease in participation clearly suggests a significant shift toward earlier retirement ages since 1950. This shift, coupled with sharp increases in life expectancy at older ages over the same period, has resulted in a significant lengthening of the typical period of retirement. For example, life expectancy at age sixty rose from 17 years in 1950 to 22.5 years in 2004 (Arias, 2007), suggesting that the duration of retirement has grown by at least that much. Simply put, retirement has become a much longer and more important phase of life.

This sharp postwar decline for men aged fifty-five to sixty-four mirrors an earlier decline in labor force participation among men aged sixty-five and older. Economic historian Dora Costa has shown that the participation rate of men in this older group was over 75 percent in 1880 but down to 50 percent by 1950, a drop she attributes primarily to rising income (Costa, 1998). Explanations for the more recent decline in participation have focused on the role of Social Security and private pensions.

This recent decline in labor force participation of older men in the United States is quite modest compared with that seen in many other developed countries. In France, for example, participation of men aged sixty to sixty-four fell from over 70 percent in 1960 to less than 20 percent in 1995 (Gruber and Wise, 1999). Currently, older men in the United States are more likely to be working than their counterparts in many but not all other developed countries. In 2008, for example, the participation rate for U.S. men in this age cohort was 13 percentage points higher than the average for the European Union but 14 points lower than for Japan.[2]

U.S. women show a strikingly different trend in labor force participation over the same period. The participation rate for women of all ages, including older women, more than doubled, from 24 percent in 1948 to 59 percent in 2008. This large increase during the postwar era can be traced to factors such as changing social norms, declining fertility rates, and increased demand for women's labor. Interestingly, a closer look at the data reveals a pause in women's rising participation in the 1970s and early 1980s, at exactly the same time when men's participation was falling the most rapidly. It may be that the same factors driving down men's participation during this period also held down the increase in women's participation, though this suggestion has yet to be corroborated.

We also examine participation rates by exact age, focusing on the period 2000 through 2007. Patterns for men and women are quite similar, with men roughly 10 percentage points more likely to be in the labor force at any given age.[3] At age fifty-five, more than three-quarters of individuals (including both men and women) are in the labor force. This proportion declines steadily until age sixty-one, when about 60 percent of the population is in the labor force. It drops more precipitously thereafter, perhaps because Social Security benefits become available at

2. Statistics downloaded from www.oecd.org/statistics (November 19, 2009).

3. This figure and those that follow are based on authors' calculations using the March Current Population Survey, a data set we describe more fully in chapter 3.

age sixty-two. By age sixty-five, only one-third of the population is in the labor force, and by age sixty-nine the proportion drops to less than one-quarter.

To determine if there are certain ages at which workers are particularly likely to exit the labor force, we calculated the drop in labor force participation rates that takes place at each age. For instance, the labor force participation rate is 61.8 percent at age sixty and 59.4 percent at age sixty-one. This means that the rate dropped 2.4 percentage points between the two ages, or 3.9 percent from the baseline rate at age sixty (100*2.4/61.8).

These age-specific drops in labor force participation can proxy for a retirement rate. They do not actually measure retirements because they do not track the age at which individuals withdrew from the labor force over time. Instead, these drops reflect the labor market behavior of different age cohorts of older workers at the same point in time. Although not the same as a "retirement rate," the idea is similar enough to treat it as a "simulated retirement rate" for the purposes of the present discussion. In chapter 3, we improve upon this approach and report the results of a similar analysis of microdata that does track individuals over time.

Simulated retirement rates by age for 2000 through 2007 show sharp spikes at ages sixty-two and sixty-five (see figure 2-1, which pools the data for men and women because the patterns are fairly similar). These spikes suggest Social Security may play a role in retirement decisions, because benefits are first available at age sixty-two and workers have traditionally been eligible to receive their full Social Security benefits at age sixty-five. Other factors may contribute to the age sixty-five spike, such as the availability of Medicare beginning at that age.

When the age-specific simulated retirement rates for the 1980s, 1990s, and the 2000s (through 2007) are compared (figure 2-2), it is clear that turning sixty-five has had a gradually decreasing impact on labor force participation, as rates at that age dropped from about 25 percent in the 1980s to 18 percent in the 2000s. Furthermore, the increase in the spike at age sixty-two between the 1980s and 1990s suggests that some of the

Figure 2-1. *Simulated Retirement Rates, by Age, 2000–07*

Simulated retirement rates

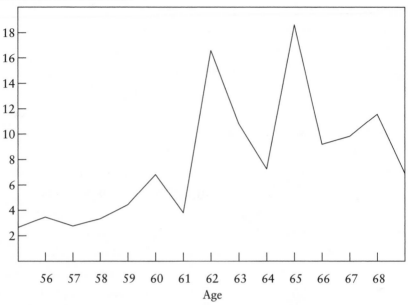

Source: Authors' calculations from March Current Population Surveys.

labor force withdrawal previously occurring at age sixty-five may now be occurring at age sixty-two. In the 2000s, however, the rates at every age are lower than they were in the 1980s. This fact coupled with the rising labor force participation rate described earlier suggests that more people are retiring in their seventies and beyond.[4]

In sum, labor force participation rates for older men dropped sharply from the 1950s through the 1980s but have leveled off and even increased somewhat since then. By contrast, rates for women of all ages, including older women, have increased during this period. Both men and women are likely to withdraw from the labor force at precisely

4. This is not shown in figure 2-2 because the number of workers at each age past age sixty-nine is fairly small and causes our estimates to be less precise.

Figure 2-2. *Trends in Simulated Retirement Rates, by Age*

Simulated retirement rates

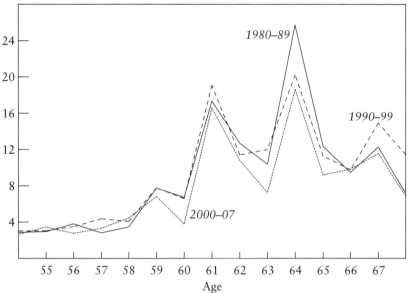

Source: Authors' calculations from March Current Population Surveys.

sixty-two and sixty-five, which could (at least in part) reflect the impact of Social Security.

Past Research

Research into retirement has been extensive over the past thirty years owing to the availability of two extremely useful sets of data: the Retirement History Survey (1969–79) and the Health and Retirement Study (1992–present). Each of these surveys followed a group of older individuals over time, interviewing them every two years during the period when many were retiring.

Much of this research deals with the role of Social Security and pensions or with the role of health and health insurance. Since the literature is reviewed in more detail elsewhere, we present only a brief summary of what is known about how workers make retirement decisions.[5] We also discuss the far fewer studies on the effects of labor markets and stock markets, which are more directly related to our analysis. First, however, it is essential to explain the key institutional features of Social Security and private pensions by way of background information.

Institutional Features of Social Security and Private Pensions

Eligibility for Social Security benefits is widespread but not universal among individuals nearing retirement age. In order to be eligible, an individual must have worked at least ten years (more precisely, forty quarters) in covered employment.[6] In 2006, 72 percent of the U.S. population between the ages of fifty-five and fifty-nine met this requirement.[7]

A retired worker's monthly Social Security benefit depends in part on how old the worker is when he or she begins to receive benefits. An eligible worker may claim benefits as early as age sixty-two but will receive a higher monthly benefit if he or she waits until a later age. The adjustment for delayed claiming is such that the total benefits received over the worker's life will be roughly the same regardless of when the worker claims. Traditionally, workers who claim at age sixty-two have their monthly benefit reduced by 20 percent relative to what they would have

---

5. For a comprehensive review of the research on Social Security and pensions, see Feldstein and Liebman (2002); for similar reviews of the research on health and health insurance, see Lumsdaine and Mitchell (1999) and Currie and Madrian (1999).

6. Virtually all sectors of the U.S. economy are currently subject to Social Security taxation, with some state and local employees being the most significant category of exempt workers (in these cases, they are covered by their own pension plans). In the past, however, some other sectors were not covered by Social Security either.

7. Authors' calculations, based on number of covered workers reported in Social Security Administration (2008) and population estimates from the U.S. Census (www.census.gov/popest/national/asrh/NC-EST2006-sa.html [December 17, 2009]). The share of the population that is not eligible for Social Security could include those who have worked primarily in noncovered employment as well as those with little to no work experience.

received if they had claimed at the "normal retirement age" of sixty-five. This discount is increasing over time to 30 percent as the normal retirement age slowly rises to age sixty-seven.

A retired worker's Social Security benefit also depends on his or her lifetime earnings. The benefit formula, which uses the worker's thirty-five best years of earnings, is progressive.[8] This means that benefits are larger for high-income workers in absolute dollar terms, but higher for low-income workers as a share of average earnings. For a typical worker who claims at age sixty-five, Social Security replaces 42 percent of average lifetime earnings, versus 56 percent for a low-wage worker (Martin and Weaver, 2005). The average monthly amount for all beneficiaries who first claimed benefits in 2007 was $1,070, although this would have been nearly $150 higher if all workers had claimed at the normal retirement age (Social Security Administration, 2008).

Any older individual who is the spouse, divorced spouse, or surviving spouse of an eligible worker is entitled to a dependent benefit (equal to 50 percent of the worker's benefit, or 100 percent in the case of surviving spouses, and also subject to reduction for early claiming). Individuals who are "dually entitled" as both a retired worker and dependent receive the larger of the benefits to which they are entitled, not both. Finally, all beneficiaries receive annual cost-of-living adjustments so that their benefits will keep up with inflation over time.

In addition to qualifying for Social Security, many workers are covered by private pension plans. Pension plans fall into two main categories: defined benefit plans and defined contribution plans. In the former type of plan, the benefit amount is calculated by a formula and depends on the worker's earnings history and age at initial benefit claim, much as with Social Security. In the latter type of plan, often referred to as a 401(k)-type plan (so named after the relevant section of the tax code), the employer, the employee, or both make contributions that are invested (as the employee specifies, but from a menu of options chosen by the firm),

8. Past years' earnings are brought up to today's dollars by applying a wage index to capture the general increase in the standard of living since the wages were earned.

and the ultimate benefit amount depends on both the contributions and investment returns, as well as the way in which the employee chooses to spend down these assets in retirement. Over the past twenty-five years, many firms have shifted from defined benefit to defined contribution plans. In 1985, for example, 80 percent of full-time employees of medium and large firms had a defined benefit plan versus only 33 percent in 2008.[9]

Research on Social Security and Pensions

As already mentioned, previous research into retirement is vast, encompassing many methodologies, perhaps the simplest being to compare changes over time in Social Security and retirement behavior. This comparison would show that men's labor force participation dropped at the same time that Social Security benefits were becoming much more generous and ubiquitous: between 1950 and 2008, the average monthly benefit amount rose fourfold (beyond the increase needed to keep up with inflation), and there was a similar jump in the number of new retired worker beneficiaries.[10] To be sure, this is far from compelling evidence of the reasons behind retirement decisions, as the coincidence of these changes does not prove that one caused the other. However, it was an important springboard for further analyses.

More rigorous, subsequent studies of aggregate behavior discovered that the spike in retirement at age sixty-two emerged only after the age of benefit eligibility was lowered from sixty-five to sixty-two in 1961 (Burtless and Moffitt, 1986) and found "no other institutional or economic reasons for the spike" (Hurd, 1990). This suggests that the structure of Social Security may play a key role in workers' retirement decisions.

9. Statistics taken from the Employee Benefit Research Institute (EBRI) Databook on Employee Benefits (www.ebri.com/publications/books/index.cfm?fa=databook [December 17, 2009]).

10. Authors' calculation from Social Security Administration (2008), tables 6.A.1 and 6.A.2.

Some of the most striking evidence of this role comes from a comparative study of the rewards/penalties for continued work beyond the first age of benefit eligibility in a dozen developed countries (Gruber and Wise, 1999). Eligible workers in many countries receive little or no increase in the monthly benefit in return for delayed claiming and thus are in effect penalized for working. The researchers found that there is a striking relationship between the size of the penalty and the share of older men in the country who work—in fact, differences in these penalties can explain 80 percent of the differences across countries in older men's labor force participation rates.

Many studies based on U.S. workers similarly conclude that Social Security affects retirement. Coile and Gruber (2007), for example, show that individuals who receive a greater reward for continued work owing to their particular earnings history or family structure are less likely to retire. Defined benefit pensions, which, like Social Security, typically specify early and normal retirement ages and often provide very strong incentives to retire at particular ages, have also been shown to be important determinants of retirement decisions (Stock and Wise, 1990).

In addition, the recent increase in men's labor force participation has been attributed in part to changes in Social Security rules, such as the increase in the normal retirement age (Gustman and Steinmeier, 2008), and to the shift to defined contribution style pension plans (Friedberg and Webb, 2005). Despite the consensus that Social Security and pensions affect retirement decisions, the portion of the decline in men's labor force participation that can be explained by the expansion of Social Security and private pensions is uncertain (Feldstein and Liebman, 2002) and may be fairly small (Diamond and Gruber, 1999).

Research on Health and Health Insurance

In the vast literature on how workers' health and access to health insurance affects their retirement decisions, some of the earliest analyses were concerned with distinguishing these effects from those of factors that interested them more, such as wages (Lambrinos, 1981). However, the effect of health on retirement eventually became the focus of much investigation in its own right.

A key question in this line of research is how to measure health. Perhaps the simplest measure is self-reported health status (whether the worker is in excellent, good, fair, or poor health). Several early studies found poor health to be associated with early retirement (Sammartino, 1987), but early retirees also reported themselves to be in worse health than one might expect from more objective measures of their health, such as the presence of chronic and acute conditions or difficulties with activities of daily living (Bazzoli, 1985). This suggested that retirees' reported health status might be affected by their retirement status, which would obscure the causal effect of health on retirement.

As a result, attention quickly turned to more objective measures of health's effect on retirement (Anderson and Burkhauser, 1985). The evidence based on these more objective measures along with that from self-reports suggests that poor health is correlated with early retirement regardless of how health is measured (Lumsdaine and Mitchell, 1999).

The research into health insurance, which dates back to the mid-1990s, suggests that it may be another key factor in workers' retirement decisions. In the United States, virtually all individuals aged sixty-five or older receive health insurance through Medicare, while the vast majority of insured individuals under that age obtain coverage through their employer or a family member's employer. Workers who retire before age sixty-five may continue to receive health insurance from their employer, but this arrangement is becoming more rare: only 29 percent of large employers (those with more than 500 workers) and 13 percent of all private employers offered such benefits in 2006, down from 38 and 22 percent, respectively, in 1997 (Fronstin, 2007). Individuals may purchase health insurance themselves, but such policies have been notoriously expensive because insurers feared that these individuals were at a higher risk of having large medical expenses. Insurance may have been unobtainable for those with certain health conditions. Recently enacted national health care reform legislation may resolve this problem.

The substantial impact of health insurance on retirement has been demonstrated by a variety of methods. By some estimates, the availability of employer-provided retiree health insurance increases the probability of retirement by 30 to 80 percent and reduces the average retirement age by six to twenty-four months (Gruber and Madrian, 1995; Blau and Gilleskie, 2001). Continuation of coverage laws, which allow workers to buy into their employer's health insurance plan at cost for a period of time after leaving the job, increases the probability of retirement by 30 percent (Gruber and Madrian, 1995). The fact that simply providing employees with an opportunity to purchase coverage has such a large effect underlines the importance of health insurance in the retirement decision for some workers.

Research on Stock Markets and Labor Markets

Since the retirement literature of the past three decades is concerned largely with the effects of Social Security, pensions, health, and health insurance, it is of little help in assessing the effect of the current economic crisis on retirement. As we highlighted earlier, public opinion seems to be that workers will postpone retirement owing to losses they have suffered in stock and housing markets. Though rather small, the literature on the effect of these markets on retirement may provide some clues to the validity of this notion.

The stock market boom of the 1990s drew some economists to consider how retirement might be affected both by the stock market and by wealth more generally. This relationship is difficult to study because it is difficult to determine causation. Suppose a person plans to retire early and saves a lot to make that possible. When he does retire early, his wealth may have no bearing on his retirement decision for he may simply be realizing his plan. In this case little can be learned about how someone else (or indeed, how this individual) might react if suddenly handed a lump sum of money, which is more to the point. The appeal of studying unexpected changes to wealth, such as those generated by a sharp rise or fall in the stock market, is that they may provide an opportunity to estimate the true effect of wealth on retirement.

So far, the research in this area is limited, and findings are mixed (see the appendix for a summary of the data, methods, and findings). Several researchers concluded that individuals who experienced large unexpected capital gains during the boom of the late 1990s retired earlier than other individuals (Sevak, 2001; Coronado and Perozek, 2003). However, subsequent studies have cast doubt on those findings (Coile and Levine, 2006; Hurd, Reti, and Rohwedder, 2009). Fundamentally, the size of such gains would depend on the amounts of stock held, and individuals with large stockholdings may be different from other people. For example, they may be better at planning or have strong preferences to retire early. When they are observed retiring earlier than other individuals during a period of large stock market gains, it could be the effect of the capital gains, but it could also be the result of these other differences. Unfortunately, it is very difficult to untangle the two.[11]

In first approaching this problem (Coile and Levine, 2006), we suggested that the stock market boom and bust experienced during the years 1995 through 2002 may provide a solution. The boom and bust together enable one to conduct a sort of double experiment (sometimes called a natural experiment or quasi experiment). If those groups that were more affected by stock market fluctuations (stockholders) were more likely to retire during the boom period and also less likely to retire during the bust period, this would be fairly convincing evidence that the market was driving retirement decisions, as it is difficult to think of another factor that could explain this pattern. We failed to find evidence of this pattern. Similarly, Hurd and his colleagues (2009) failed to find any difference in how stockholders and non-stockholders revise their expected retirement dates

11. Note that in their attempt to disentangle the two, Coronado and Perozek (2003) find that being a stockholder is associated with retiring six months earlier than expected compared with being a non-stockholder, while each additional $100,000 in unexpected gains (a relatively large amount) is associated with retiring only two weeks earlier than expected. The fact that being a stockholder is so much more important than the specific amount of the gain indicates it is indeed essential to use a strategy that controls for underlying differences in those with and without capital gains.

during periods of boom and bust. In subsequent research (Coile and Levine, 2009), we incorporated more recent data and looked more carefully at whether people respond to short-term or long-term stock market returns (for the methods and results, see chapters 3 and 4, respectively).

Little work has yet been done on how housing markets affect retirement. The results of our own research here (Coile and Levine, 2009) are presented in chapter 5.

The effect of labor markets on retirement has not received much attention, either. Results to date indicate that job loss is an important phenomenon for older workers. Farber (2005) reports that more than 10 percent of workers aged fifty-five to sixty-four lost their jobs during the period 2001–03. Job loss appears to have significant long-term effects on older workers' employment and wages. Chan and Stevens (1999) estimate that the employment rate of displaced older workers several years after the job loss is 25 percentage points lower than that of a comparable group of nondisplaced workers, and the typical displaced worker who does find a new job is earning 20 percent less than at his old job.

The fact that older workers face a considerable risk of job loss and difficulty finding an equivalent job afterward suggests that labor market conditions may affect retirement decisions. Yet this link has been by and large overlooked, even though a weak labor market can limit an individual's ability to continue to work at older ages in much the same way as poor health.

Our own findings on the effect of labor market conditions on retirement (Coile and Levine, 2007, 2009) are discussed in chapter 6. Briefly, it appears that the probability of retirement increases with the unemployment rate, and that this effect is concentrated among retirement transitions that occur with a reported spell of unemployment or with receipt of unemployment insurance (UI) benefits. This effect is present starting only at age sixty-one, as workers approach the age of Social Security eligibility. In addition, there is no evidence that the unemployment rate has a bigger effect on retirement in states with more generous UI benefits. Taken together, these findings suggest that older workers may rely more on Social Security than UI to weather labor market shocks.

The role of labor market conditions has also been explored by Hallberg (2008), who shows that retirement transitions by Swedish workers increase when their industries have periods of low employment compared with the industry trend, and by von Wachter (2007), who finds that both industry-level employment and state-level unemployment rates affect the labor force participation of older workers. Other studies—including those of Black and Liang (2005), Friedberg and others (2008), and Munnell and others (2008)—use different methods but obtain similar conclusions. All of these studies are also summarized in the appendix. Thus evidence to date that labor market conditions are an important determinant of retirement is strong enough to call for further study of their effects.

3 | Detecting the Impact of Market Conditions

Since the purpose of this book is to investigate the influence of stock market, housing market, and labor market conditions on retirement decisions and subsequent retiree well-being, it is essential to explain how one does that. The procedure turns out to be rather complicated.

To begin, it requires information on workers' retirement decisions. Many factors come into play when an individual is contemplating retirement. Conditions in stock, housing, and labor markets are merely a few of them. As important as these conditions may be, we believe that for most workers they are not the primary determinants of retirement. Rather, retirement decisions are largely driven by the extent to which individuals enjoy working in general and their job in particular, as well as by their family situation, health status, and anticipated pension and Social Security benefits, among other things. Since market conditions are likely to have a smaller influence on retirement than these other factors, it is necessary to observe the behavior of a large number of individuals approaching retirement in order to find such an effect.

Even a large database will shed no light on market effects if all the data come from one point in time, since market conditions at any such point are unchanging. Currently the labor market is weak, stock and house prices are low, and individuals are retiring at a certain rate.

Assuming that today's retirement rates are relatively low by historical standards, to what extent are current market conditions responsible? This question cannot be addressed without observing how retirement patterns change as market conditions change.

Another factor to consider is that market conditions tend not to change rapidly. Although the stock market fluctuates all the time, much of that is noise. Over the past three decades, the United States has experienced four recessions as well as two sizable bull markets and two major stock market crashes. Booms and busts in the housing market occur only over long periods of time as well. This means one needs to observe waves of individuals approaching retirement over a long period of time in order to determine whether changes in market conditions affect the decision to retire.

Obtaining these formidable data is just the first part of the process; the harder part is using them to establish whether rising unemployment or falling stock and housing prices cause individuals to change their behavior. Just because two things happen at the same time does not mean that one necessarily caused the other. The goal of any well-designed statistical analysis is to determine whether an observed relationship between two events is a causal one. We believe our methodological approach satisfies this goal, as we describe later in the chapter.

What Data Do We Use?

Our analysis requires data for a large number of individuals collected over a long period of time but also specific kinds of data related to the retirement decision and to retiree well-being. For the retirement decision, we need data on the labor market activity of individuals around traditional retirement ages. Here we rely on thirty years of data from the March Current Population Survey. For retiree well-being, we need data on the well-being of older individuals who are past traditional retirement ages. Here we rely on income data drawn from the 2000 Census and the 2001–07 American Community Surveys.

The March Current Population Survey

The Current Population Survey (CPS) is perhaps the most important survey of labor market activity in the United States. Administered monthly by the Bureau of Labor Statistics, the CPS is used to generate estimates of the monthly unemployment rate. Hence the survey's questions are designed to reveal the nature of each respondent's involvement in the labor market in the week before the survey. The survey also obtains information on a number of demographic characteristics of the respondent, including race, ethnicity, age, marital status, number of children, educational attainment, and, starting in 1978, state of residence. We use this geographic information along with data on state-level house prices and unemployment rates in our analyses of housing and labor market effects.

In March of each year, the Annual Social and Economic Supplement (formerly known as the Annual Demographic Survey) is administered as a supplement to the CPS. This supplement provides a wealth of information on the labor market activity of respondents in the preceding calendar year, including weeks worked, usual hours worked per week, weeks spent looking for work, and the like.

We draw on the information in this supplement to construct a measure of retirement. Difficult as it is to define retirement, as noted in chapter 2, the nature of the CPS data forces us to restrict our definition to complete labor force withdrawal. Specifically, we take retirement to occur when an older worker reports working or looking for work in the preceding calendar year for at least thirteen weeks but is out of the labor force on the March survey date. If the worker's reported labor market activity occurred consecutively starting at the beginning of the preceding calendar year (an assumption we have no way to verify), then we can interpret this to mean that a person is retired if he or she was working in March and is out of the labor force by the following March. In this sense, we can use our data to calculate something like an annual retirement rate, where a year spans the period from one March to the next rather than the course of a calendar year.

We concentrate on workers between the ages of fifty-five and sixty-nine, as they are more likely to retire in any given year. Despite the relatively small slice of the population that this group represents, the size of the CPS is large enough to generate a large sample of workers at risk of retirement. Total sample sizes in the March CPS have varied over time, but run about 130,000 to 215,000 people a year. Looking at March CPS data from 1980 through 2008, we obtained data for almost 600,000 individuals between the ages of fifty-five and sixty-nine, just over half of whom were in the labor force thirteen or more weeks in the year before the survey. On average, 9 percent of workers exited the labor force each year of our study period.

The U.S. Census and the American Community Surveys

In accordance with the Constitution, the federal government must conduct a census every decade to obtain a complete and accurate count of the population. This is done to enable the government to determine how many members of the House of Representatives to allocate to each state. Although statistical analyses on retirement outcomes were (surprisingly!) not part of the constitutional mandate, modern censuses also provide the necessary information for this use.

During the Census, most households are required to complete a "short form" asking them to list their members and to provide very limited additional data for each. Five percent of the population is asked to complete a "long form" calling for greater detail about the household and its members. Questions about the household ask whether the residence is owned or rented, the level of their mortgage payment or rent, the physical characteristics of the dwelling, and the like; questions about its members pertain to demographic characteristics, educational attainment, and, important for this discussion, labor market activity and levels of income by type. Because it samples 5 percent of the country's population of 300 million, the long form produces data on a very large number of respondents, roughly 15 million people in each census year.

The American Community Survey (ACS) is a new source of data recently developed in response to the need for population data in the interval between the decennial censuses. It is modeled on the Census Bureau's long form and calls for very similar information.[1] When the survey was proposed and designed, it was to cover 1 percent of the population each year (roughly 3 million respondents). Between 2000 and 2004, the survey was piloted on smaller samples, and by 2005 that design was fully implemented. Still, in the earlier years hundreds of thousands of respondents were sampled. We restrict our attention to the 2001–07 ACS surveys. Combining these two sources provides us with continuous data between 2000 and 2007.[2]

We rely on census and ACS data for our analysis of the well-being of older workers after they have retired. Both provide extensive information on the income received by every individual in the household in the past calendar year. Each individual is asked the same set of income questions, and the income reported by each person is recorded separately. The survey collects data on income from wages and salaries, self-employment, investments, Social Security, Supplemental Security Income (SSI), public assistance, private pensions, and other income sources.

The amounts of income that an individual receives from these sources are easier to determine in some cases than in others. Wages and salaries, Social Security, and pension benefits are all likely to be direct-deposited in the amount of the individual's benefit. For other sources of income, particularly investment income, it may be difficult to distinguish who received it, especially if the underlying investment is jointly held. The survey questionnaire guides respondents to report "appropriate shares

---

1. Indeed, the Minnesota Population Center provides unified Census/ACS extracts through its IPUMS USA project; we use those data. For more detail, see Ruggles and others (2009). These data are available at http://usa.ipums.org/usa/.

2. In theory, one could include data from earlier census years, such as 1990 and 1980. However, it is somewhat awkward to work with a sample that consists of continuous data for 2000–07 and only sporadic (once a decade) data from earlier years. Our sample includes individuals in the years 1920–36 (and thus aged seventy-one to eighty in survey years 2000–07, or aged seventy to seventy-nine in the preceding year for which they report income), which represents a big enough time span to provide significant variation in the stock and labor market conditions around the time of retirement.

for each person." If this is not possible, respondents are to attribute all such income to one person and none to the other.

In our analysis of retiree well-being, we focus on the impact of economic conditions around the time of retirement on individual income. Different members of the same household may reach retirement age at different times. It is the economic conditions at the time of each individual's own retirement that affects his or her own income in retirement. Reports of personal income are therefore central to our analysis.

We should also make clear that when we substitute income for well-being, we are doing so out of practical considerations. An individual's well-being should obviously be very broadly defined to incorporate any number of specific outcomes—income is simply the easiest of these to measure. Our focus on income is somewhat at odds with an important economic principle, namely, that individuals value the stream of consumption that income brings about and not the income itself. Although we agree with this view in theory, we also recognize that no consumption data exist that would allow us to use this as an outcome in our analysis. Since income and consumption are strongly related, however, we believe the effect of market conditions on overall individual well-being can be detected from the receipt of income.

We draw on the 2000 Census and seven ACS samples beginning in 2001 for income data spanning the years 1999–2006. These data were collected from about 1.68 million respondents between the ages of seventy-one and eighty.[3] Their reported income refers to amounts received in the preceding calendar year, when the respondents were between the

3. Alexander, Davern, and Stevenson (2010) caution that age and sex variables in the 2000 Census and some subsequent American Community Surveys may contain some miscoded data owing to erroneous disclosure-avoidance procedures. Although the evidence they provide is disturbing, these problems do not appear to have a substantial impact on our analysis. In theory, if age is not always reported correctly, this could mar our calculation of the unemployment rate at age sixty-two and thus bias our estimates (toward zero, if the reporting errors are random). However, we do not believe this is a problem for us because we find that the unemployment rate at age sixty-two affects subsequent retiree income for the less educated but not the more educated; this pattern cannot be explained by meas-

ages of seventy and seventy-nine. All income figures are adjusted to 2007 dollars. Of these respondents, we restrict our attention to the well-being of those who have withdrawn from the labor force. This limits our sample to 1.49 million respondents in this age group. We also make one further sample restriction. For reasons described more fully in chapter 7, we focus on the incomes of men. Our final sample thus consists of about 600,000 male retirees in their seventies.[4]

Why Two Different Data Sources?

Since the CPS and the Census/ACS contain similar data, one might reasonably ask why we rely only on the CPS for our analysis of retirement and on the Census and ACS for our analysis of retirement income. The answer is that each source offers different advantages for each exercise. In the case of retirement, we wish to explore how market conditions in a given period affect retirement decisions in that same period. The CPS enables us to observe market fluctuations over a period of thirty years and thereby better determine how those fluctuations alter retirement behavior. By contrast, the Census/ACS data span a period of only eight years. Since markets fluctuate less over this shorter period, the data therein are poorer indicators of how changing market conditions alter retirement decisions.

In examining income in retirement, however, we are relating current income for a group of individuals between the ages of seventy and seventy-nine to the market conditions that existed around the time of their retirement. Suppose we are interested in market conditions at the time those workers reach age sixty-two (why we might choose this age is explained in chapter 7). If in each survey year we focus on individuals between the ages of seventy-one and eighty (reporting income at ages

---

urement error and is quite sensible given our other findings (for example, that less-educated workers are more likely to retire early in response to a weak labor market than are more-educated workers).

4. Of this group, 285,000 respondents were from the 2000 Census, about 27,000 were from each year of the ACS in 2001–04, and 67,000 to 70,000 were from each year of the ACS in 2005–07.

seventy to seventy-nine), they would be sixty-two in many different years. In the 2000 Census, for instance, individuals seventy-one to eighty in the year 2000 were sixty-two in the years 1982 through 1991. In the 2007 ACS, individuals seventy-one to eighty were sixty-two in the years 1989 through 1998. In essence, we are able to observe income in retirement for those who were age sixty-two between the years 1982 and 1998. This provides a seventeen-year window through which to observe varying market conditions. This large window combined with the very large number of retirees in the Census and ACS samples makes these surveys a better source of data for this exercise.

Why Use Past Data to Analyze the Current Crisis?

As discussed earlier, the effect of market conditions on retirement cannot be determined from data collected at one point in time, since low retirement rates today could be related to other factors besides market conditions. Retirement behavior has to be examined over several decades to assess whether changes in market conditions have led to changes in retirement behavior. The estimates from this analysis can then be used to predict the effect of the current crisis on retirement, as we do in chapter 8. In using historical data to forecast the impact of current events, we are following standard practice in empirical research.

Statistics on Retirement Rates and Income in Retirement

At this point, a few words are in order about retirement patterns by age and over time, and about the sources and levels of income that individuals use to fund their retirement.

Retirement Patterns

The long time span of CPS data makes it possible to discern patterns in retirement behavior over time, as well as patterns by age at a particular point in time. We also examine patterns of retirement by level of education, a marker of socioeconomic status, because market conditions may affect different groups of workers differently.

The relevant statistic here is the "retirement rate." It is formally defined as the share of all workers in the labor force for thirteen or more weeks in the preceding year who have withdrawn completely from the labor force by the March survey date.[5] To elaborate, if 100 workers started on the job the preceding year (or to be slightly more technical, if 100 workers reported being in the labor force for at least thirteen weeks last year, which we assume means they were still working or looking for work in March) and 10 of them withdrew from the labor force by March of the current year, then the retirement rate would be 10 percent. Note that this means there are now only 90 individuals in the labor force at the start of the next year. If another 10 workers exit the labor force by the following March, then the next year's retirement rate would be 11.1 percent: 100 (10/90).

Figure 3-1 presents retirement rates over time for the full sample of workers between the ages of fifty-five and sixty-nine in our CPS data. Through the early 1990s, retirement rates held reasonably steady at about 10 percent. After that, the rates trend strongly downward, reaching a level of just over 6 percent in more recent years.[6] This pattern is consistent with the upward trend in the labor force participation rate of older workers over this period, as reported in chapter 2.

As figure 3-1 also shows, the retirement rate may vary, blipping up or down half a percent or more from year to year, movements which look like noise when viewed against longer-term trends. This suggests that it may be difficult to estimate the effect of changes in market conditions on retirement simply by looking for cyclical movements in the retirement rate. In the years in which there was a recession, for instance, does the retirement rate look higher or lower? The "evidence" in this

5. Demographers would call this statistic a hazard rate. It resembles mortality rates in that it calculates the number of "deaths" among those "alive" at the beginning of a period. The hazard rate has many applications beyond mortality, including divorce and the end of unemployment spells.

6. One concern regarding this conclusion is that baby boomers began to turn fifty-five in 2001, which would lower the average age of the sample of workers to fifty-five to sixty-nine. When we experimented with age-adjusting this retirement trend, we found that the underlying trend is still very strong.

Figure 3-1. *Trend in the Retirement Rate, Ages Fifty-Five to Sixty-Nine*

Annual percent of retiring workers, 55 to 69

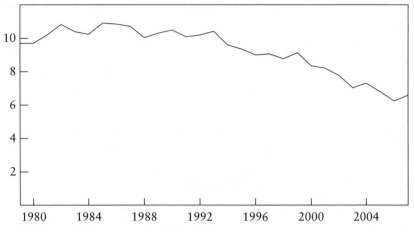

Source: Authors' calculations from March Current Population Surveys.

figure does not readily point to any such change. The early 1980s, the early 1990s, and the early 2000s were all periods of suppressed economic activity, yet there does not appear to be any difference in retirement rates in those periods. In view of the annual noise in the data, any effect would have to be rather large to be detected. There are no such large effects here.

By combining data for workers of all ages (fifty-five to sixty-nine) and exploring trends in retirement over time, figure 3-1 ignores the impact of age on retirement. Figure 3-2 reverses this approach, ignoring the impact of time by combining data for all years (1979–2007) and focusing on the role that age plays in retirement decisions. Here there is a general upward trend, indicating that the likelihood that a worker will retire over the course of a year rises as workers age. This is hardly surprising, as individuals may find work increasingly taxing as they age, or they may simply reach the age at which they had planned to retire in ever-greater numbers. About 5 percent of workers in their mid-fifties retire over the course of a year, while more than 15 percent in their late sixties do so.

Figure 3-2. *Retirement Rates, by Age, 1979–2007*

Annual percent of retiring workers

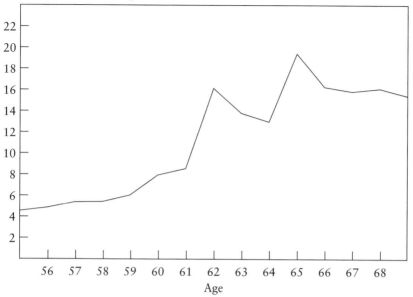

Source: Authors' calculations from March Current Population Surveys.

More striking are the clear spikes in this age pattern. Workers appear to have higher retirement rates precisely at ages sixty-two and sixty-five than one might expect solely on the basis of their age. At age sixty-one, 8.5 percent of workers retire. At sixty-two, that rate almost doubles to 16 percent before falling to lower levels at ages sixty-three and sixty-four. A similar spike occurs at sixty-five. At sixty-four, 13 percent of workers choose to retire, but that rate rises to 19 percent at sixty-five, again falling somewhat after this. As noted in chapter 2, these are the kinds of data commonly used to argue that individual retirement decisions are influenced by the incentives built into private pensions and the Social Security system.

In figure 3-3, we combine the changes in retirement behavior over time with the changes that take place as workers age. In this case, we break the sample period 1979–2007 roughly into thirds and calculate the age profile in retirement rates for the 1980s, the 1990s, and the 2000s

Figure 3-3. *Retirement Trends, by Age, over the Past Three Decades*

Annual percent of retiring workers

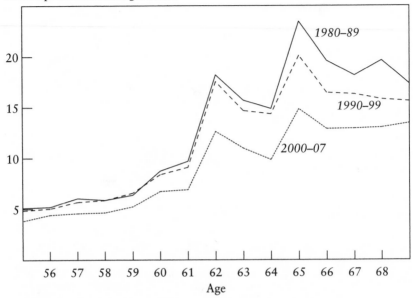

Source: Authors' calculations from March Current Population Surveys.

(through 2007). Note that retirement rates at every age are lower in the 2000s than in the earlier periods. It turns out that the overall trend toward delayed retirement apparent in figure 3-1 reflects lower retirement rates at all ages. The spikes at ages sixty-two and sixty-five may not be quite as large as in the past, but they are still rather prominent.

In figures 3-4 and 3-5, the retirement rates are reported separately for workers with different levels of education. This is an important exercise if one is to assess how market conditions affect workers of varying socioeconomic status. Clearly, education is a key element of overall socioeconomic status.

Figure 3-4 shows the time trend in retirement rates among workers aged fifty-five to sixty-nine by level of education.[7] All education groups exhibit the same overall trend over time toward delayed retirement, but

7. When we separate workers into these subgroups and estimate annual retirement rates, the level of noise becomes substantive. In order to focus on broader

Figure 3-4. *Impact of Education on Annual Retirement Trends, Ages Fifty-Five to Sixty-Nine*[a]

Annual percent of retiring workers, 55 to 69

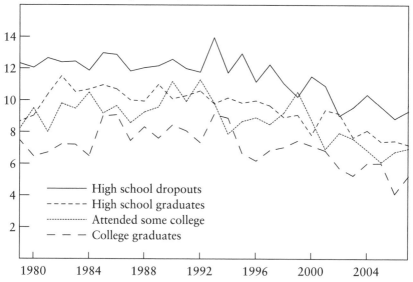

——— High school dropouts
- - - - - High school graduates
············· Attended some college
− − − College graduates

Source: Authors' calculations from March Current Population Surveys.
a. All lines represent three-year moving averages.

less-skilled workers (as defined by lower levels of education) have higher retirement rates each year. One can imagine several reasons for this: more-skilled workers are likely to enjoy higher wages, higher job satisfaction, better health, and less physically taxing jobs than less-skilled workers. Whatever the reason, college graduates retire at annual rates that are a third or more lower than those of high school dropouts.

Figure 3-5 displays age patterns in retirement rates by level of education. For the most part, the same age-specific patterns in retirement observed for all workers in figure 3-2 are evident for workers in every education group. Retirement rates rise with age, and spikes are evident at ages sixty-two and sixty-five. The most noticeable difference is the

---

trends rather than specific year-to-year fluctuations, we report three-year, backward-looking, moving averages.

Figure 3-5. *Impact of Education on Retirement Rates, by Age, 1979–2007*

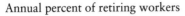
Annual percent of retiring workers

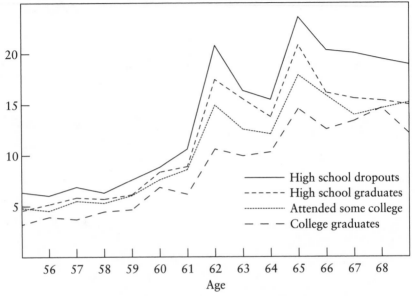

Source: Authors' calculations from March Current Population Surveys.

size of the spikes: they are quite large at both ages for less-skilled workers and somewhat moderated for more-skilled workers.

A review of these patterns is useful for our subsequent analysis because we implement methods that abstract from the differences in underlying behavior over time, by age, and, in some instances, across workers' level of education that would have occurred regardless of changes in market conditions. This should help determine whether changes in market conditions lead workers to change their retirement decisions from what they would otherwise have been at the same age, time period, and level of education.

Income in Retirement

Drawing on the Census and the ACS data for men in the years 2000–07, we examine retirees' level of total income as well as their

Table 3-1. *Mean Incomes of Seventy- to Seventy-Nine-Year-Old Retired Men, by Location in Total Personal Income Distribution*[a]

Group	Total personal	Social Security	Pension	Investment	Other
All	34,034	11,388	10,730	8,066	3,850
Bottom third	9,686	7,807	701	306	872
Middle third	23,032	12,673	6,429	2,261	1,669
Top third	68,356	13,621	24,644	21,234	8,857

Source: Authors' calculations from the 2000 Census and 2001–07 American Community Surveys.

a. Reported dollar values represent the mean for each income type in each income level and are reported in 2007 dollars.

income by source. These data represent income received in the years 1999–2006. Note, too, that these are personal income statistics, which refer to the income of the individual, not that of the entire household. We consider only those retirees who were between seventy-one and eighty on the survey date, or between seventy and seventy-nine in the preceding year, when the income was received. We also separate individuals into three equal-sized groups according to their level of income so as to observe differences in income receipt by source for individuals at each level.

As table 3-1 shows, the average male retiree in this age group receives about $34,000 a year in total personal income. This income is more or less evenly split in its sources: Social Security, pensions, and investments. Only a small amount of additional income is reported from other sources.

Table 3-1 also shows that mean levels of income rise with a retiree's position in the income distribution; those in the top, middle, and bottom third receive an average personal income of $68,356, $23,032, and $9,686 a year, respectively. Interestingly, when the sources of income are compared across groups, Social Security represents a very large share (81 percent) of total income for lower-income men, versus 55 percent and 20 percent for middle- and upper-income men, respectively.

Furthermore, lower-income households receive little income from pensions and investment: less than $1,000 from each source, on average.

Table 3-2. *Percent of Seventy- to Seventy-Nine-Year-Old Retired Men Reporting Any Income, by Location in Total Personal Income Distribution*

Group	Social Security	Pension	Investment
All	90.9	51.9	46.5
Bottom third	83.6	15.9	16.6
Middle third	95.3	64.3	47.4
Top third	93.7	74.8	74.8

Source: Authors' calculations from the 2000 Census and 2001–07 American Community Surveys.

Middle-income men receive a sizable component of their income from pensions, but even for them investment income is only $2,261 a year, on average. If investment income were cut in half, it would make a small dent in the well-being of middle-income men. Only those in the top third of the income distribution receive enough investment income for market fluctuations to have much of an impact on their well-being.

Further analysis shows that more than 90 percent of all male retirees between seventy and seventy-nine receive Social Security income, and the rates of receipt are very high throughout the income distribution (table 3-2). By contrast, pension and investment income are much less common, and the rates of receipt vary more noticeably by income category. Roughly half of the sample population receives income from these sources. Those at the bottom of the distribution are very unlikely (around 16 percent) to receive income from pensions and investments, while those at the top are very likely to do so (around 75 percent).

For those men who receive any pension or investment income, the amount received is also strongly related to one's position in the income distribution. For those in the bottom third, receipts in each category amount to less than $5,000; those in the top third collect around $30,000, on average (table 3-3). Again, the level of Social Security income is considerably more similar across income groups. This feature is by design, since the benefit formula is designed so that benefits will rise fairly slowly with earnings beyond a certain point.

Table 3-3. *Mean Incomes of Seventy- to Seventy-Nine-Year-Old Retired Men for Those Receiving Any Income, by Location in Total Personal Income Distribution*[a]

Group	Social Security	Pension	Investment
All	11,388	10,730	8,066
Bottom third	9,343	4,420	2,039
Middle third	13,299	9,998	4,804
Top third	14,533	32,927	28,418

Source: Authors' calculations from the 2000 Census and 2001–07 American Community Surveys.

a. Reported dollar values represent the mean for each income type in each income level and are reported in 2007 dollars.

Using the Data

The difficulty in establishing a causal relationship from data such as the foregoing cannot be emphasized enough. One need only recall the recent controversy surrounding the introduction of a vaccine to protect against the H1N1 virus. A major concern was whether its side effects might be worse than the disease. Some predicted an increase in the number of miscarriages, heart attacks, and other maladies with the vaccine's widespread use. Upward of 200 million doses were expected to be administered in the United States. Certainly some small fraction of those vaccinated would fall ill, and many of those would blame the vaccine.

From a public health perspective, however, the coincidence of vaccinations and adverse health events is insufficient evidence that the vaccine is to blame. Bad health outcomes occur every day regardless of vaccination programs. Every twenty-four hours, almost 2,000 people in the United States die from heart attacks, and almost 3,000 pregnant women miscarry.[8] Certainly some of those who receive vaccines will have heart attacks and some women will miscarry, but it will not necessarily be as a result of the vaccine.

8. Statistics on miscarriage are from Ventura and others (2009), those on heart attack from a CDC website (www.cdc.gov/heartDisease/statistics.htm [October 15, 2009]).

The Concept of Causality

Before causality can be established, one needs to know the counterfactual: that is, what would have happened otherwise? In the case of H1N1 vaccine, it is fairly easy to obtain that counterfactual. Since ample data are available on how many heart attacks and miscarriages typically occur in a given population, the vaccine can be blamed only if more people experience these events after its application than would otherwise be expected.

Often, however, determining the counterfactual is far more difficult. This can be demonstrated with patterns of labor force participation rates among men aged fifty-five to sixty-four since the economic crisis began in September of 2008. At that time, 70 percent of men in this age group were in the labor force. As the crisis began to unfold and the economy weakened, labor force participation rates rose, reaching 71 percent by May 2009, but then fell back to 69.6 percent in September of that year. Still, a greater proportion of men in this age group were in the labor force than at any point since the early 1980s.

These statistics might lead some to conclude that the current economic crisis is causing people to delay retirement. According to a recent Economic Policy Institute issue brief, for instance, "The higher labor force participation of workers 55 and older is at least in part a response to rising health care costs, plummeting home values, and losses in 401(k)s and individual retirement accounts, which are combining to make retirement unaffordable" (Garr, 2009).

Just as in the case of illnesses occurring after H1N1 vaccinations, however, it is impossible to establish whether changes in labor force participation rates are caused by the crisis without knowing the counterfactual. Since labor force participation of older male workers has grown steadily over the past fifteen years or so, other factors could well explain the rise, such as changing incentives built into Social Security or the growth of defined contribution pension plans. Of course, additional evidence would be required to nail down its actual cause. In any event, it appears that labor force participation rates of older men likely would still be rising in the absence of the economic crisis.

This does not mean that the economic crisis played no role in leading older workers to delay retirement and stay in the workforce longer. Rather, one cannot assume the economic crisis was the sole or leading cause simply because labor force participation has risen since the crisis began. Perhaps labor force participation should have been expected to rise by more than it has. Then in relation to the counterfactual, one could conclude that retirement has become a more common phenomenon. All in all, what this discussion demonstrates is that sophisticated statistical methods are required to attribute causality to real-world events, as we do with market conditions and their potential impact on retirement outcomes and retiree well-being.[9]

The Role of Experiments

Causal relationships are sometimes explored by means of a controlled experiment, as is common in the pharmaceutical industry when a company wants to determine the effectiveness of a new drug. Once the drug has passed some preliminary tests to make sure that it does no obvious harm to those who take it, a controlled experiment is conducted. Participants in the experiment are randomly divided into treatment and control groups; group membership is unknown to the participant. Members of the treatment group receive the new drug, and members of the control group receive a placebo.

A controlled experiment is designed around the notion of random assignment. That is, individuals are randomly assigned to treatment and control groups; the two groups will then have statistically identical characteristics. Each group has similar numbers of smokers, people with high blood pressure, people with heart disease or whatever other factors may influence health outcomes in the absence of the drug. Random

9. For the full details of our approach, see Coile and Levine (2009, 2010).

assignment makes it possible to hold constant all other differences that exist between people except for the particular intervention of interest—the use of a certain drug in this example. The control group provides the counterfactual. What would health outcomes have been were it not for the drug? As a result, any observable differences in health outcomes between groups can be attributed to the drug itself.

One might find this approach appropriate for testing drug effectiveness in laboratory settings, but not so useful for the real world of social science. Yet controlled experiments are not uncommon in these types of settings, as is clear from the array of experimental evidence on the influence of programs dedicated to early childhood education, job training, and other social endeavors.

Even so, it is difficult to imagine ever implementing an experiment to test the relationship between an economic crisis and retirement decisions. In theory, this would entail randomly assigning older workers into environments in which they either experience an economic crisis or not. Retirement decisions in the two types of environments would then be compared and the individuals followed through time to measure their well-being in retirement. The logistical and ethical issues bound to arise in such an exercise clearly make this technique impractical—even to the point of being ridiculous. Nevertheless, it is important to keep in mind that this is the approach that we are trying to emulate.

Using Alternative Statistical Methods to Simulate This Approach

To do so, we must rely on more sophisticated statistical techniques in the analysis. The methods used in examining the effect of market conditions on retirement decisions and on well-being in retirement are similar, but not identical. Here we focus on the former. The modifications to this approach needed for our analysis of retirement income are discussed in chapter 7.

In analyzing retirement decisions, we are fortunate to have access to data over a very long period of time (1979 to 2007). This enables us to observe several full cycles in labor market activity, stock market returns, and housing prices. It also enables us to gauge what changes in retirement behavior over time can be explained by ongoing trends and what changes amount to period-specific effects that deviate from the longer-term trends. The objective here is to determine whether the period-specific changes in retirement behavior occur during periods in which market conditions are relatively strong or weak.

As evident in figure 3-2, retirement rates vary dramatically with age, rising gradually with age but jumping sharply at certain ages. If a population's age patterns change (because of the aging of the baby boom, for example) and the change happens to coincide with changing market conditions, then one may inadvertently assume a connection between those market conditions and retirement rates. Hence it is important to examine the impact of market conditions on retirement rates when the age distribution of the retirement-eligible population is unchanging. Our statistical approach enables us to do that.

In our analysis of the impact of changing housing and labor market conditions, we also take into account differences in market conditions by geographic location. Recessions and housing slumps are sometimes worse in some locations than in others. Differences in the industrial composition of the location, the demographics of the population, and other area-specific factors that do not change much over time may also affect retirement patterns. The workforce in states with a higher percentage of manufacturing employment may retire earlier than in states with a high percentage of service employment, for instance. Unemployment rates tend to always be higher in manufacturing states regardless of business cycles. The question of interest here is whether retirement increases more in one state (say, a state with a large share of manufacturing employment) than in others if unemployment rises more in that state than in other states. Thus it is necessary to adjust for these long-standing differences in conditions across markets and determine the impact of changes in those conditions within markets. Our statistical approach enables us to do just that.

To recap, our analysis of retirement decisions draws on data for individuals who vary by year, age, and their geographic location. Market conditions change over time and, in some instances, vary across locations; furthermore, market conditions may affect individuals at different ages differently.

Our approach enables us to simulate the experimental ideal in that we are able to hold factors such as year, age, and location constant. Members exposed to strong or weak market conditions can be viewed as the treatment group and those exposed to "normal" market conditions as the control group. Although in reality these conditions occur at different times, our methods adjust for that, so one can think of them as taking place at the same time. Furthermore, members of the control and treatment groups might differ in age or might live in different places, but we introduce methods that adjust for those differences as well. The end result is something that resembles the experimental approach and enables us to adequately determine whether market conditions have a causal effect on retirement decisions.[10]

10. This is not to say that our methods are without limitations. They are certainly not perfect, but a full accounting of these issues is well beyond the scope of this book. Nevertheless, they represent a standard methodological approach that provides, perhaps, the best way to attempt to determine causality in the absence of true experimental data.

4 | *Impact of the Stock Market Crash*

If the numerous media reports and public opinion polls blaming the recent stock market crash for a decline in retirement are to hold water, several conditions must be met. First, any drop in the stock market must be large enough to potentially affect people's behavior. As any stock market watcher knows, it is not uncommon for major market indices like the S&P 500 Index or Dow Jones Industrial Average to rise or fall by several percentage points or more over the course of a week, or even within a single day. This has been especially true over the past several years, as market volatility has increased. It seems unlikely that people would change their retirement plans in response to these routine changes, but they may respond to market movements that are larger and more sustained, which represent a greater or smaller return compared with what the investor might have expected.

Second, people must have enough stock-based assets for a large drop in asset values to substantially affect their well-being. If only a small minority of the population has a substantial amount of money invested in stocks, then a dramatic market decline may induce some people to delay retirement, but there will be too few such individuals for this to translate into a large change in aggregate retirement behavior.

And third, people must actually respond to fluctuations in their stock holdings in the way that economic theory would predict. Specifically, when the market goes up by more than expected, older workers should consume some of these unanticipated capital gains in the form of leisure time and retire earlier than they otherwise would; conversely, if the market drops unexpectedly, they should retire later. Workers say that they will do this in public opinion polls, but most economists believe that actions speak louder than words and would like some concrete evidence that people actually respond to stock market fluctuations in this way. Since the current crisis is still too new to fully assess its effect, one must look at how workers have responded to market fluctuations in the past in order to answer this question.

In searching for evidence of these three conditions, we first examine stock market returns over time, to determine how large and unusual the current market decline is in comparison with historical norms. Second, we explore the stock holdings of workers now nearing retirement age and estimate the possible impact of the current market decline on their future retirement income. Third, we conduct an empirical analysis using the data and methods described in chapter 3 to assess whether there is a causal link between market fluctuations and retirement. In essence, we are comparing the effect of stock market movements on retirement for groups that were relatively more and less likely to have substantial stock holdings. To the extent that market fluctuations affect retirement, we expect those groups more likely to hold substantial stock assets to change their retirement more in response to an upswing or downturn in the market, in comparison with other groups.

Stock Market Fluctuations

Throughout our analysis, we use the Standard and Poor's 500 Index (S&P 500) as our primary measure of stock market value. This index tracks changes in the value of the 500 largest public companies in the United States, which jointly account for about 75 percent of the total U.S. equity market. The S&P 500 is widely regarded as the best indicator of the performance of the "large cap" segment of the market, as well as an excellent proxy for the performance of the market overall.

Figure 4-1. *S&P 500 Index, 1979–2009*

Index value

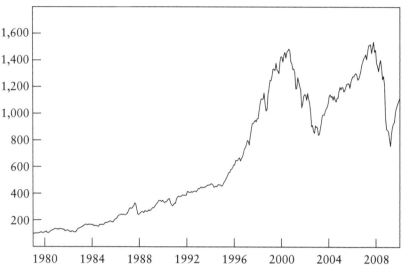

Source: S&P 500 Index Monthly Average (www.freelunch.com).

The S&P 500 is a nominal index, meaning it does not correct for the effect of inflation, so increases in the index over time will reflect both the effect of inflation and real increases in the value of the firms included in the index. As indicated in figure 4-1, the index rose steadily during the 1980s and early 1990s, with any losses—such as those experienced on "Black Monday" in October 1987—being made up within a year or two at the most. In the late 1990s, however, the value of the S&P 500 rose much more quickly. This was followed by an equally steep decline in the market starting in late 2000, when a period of speculative investment in high-technology companies known as the "dot.com bubble" came to an end. The S&P 500 Index lost more than 40 percent of its value over the next two years, while the tech-heavy NASDAQ index fell by two-thirds.

Remarkably, this dramatic cycle of boom and bust was essentially repeated in the years since then. The S&P 500 turned the corner after the dot.com crash and began to climb rapidly again starting in late 2002, hitting new all-time highs by late 2007. Unfortunately for investors, these gains turned out to be fleeting. Between late 2007 and early 2009, the S&P 500 dropped by 50 percent, to levels not seen in more than a decade. Although it is too early to say for sure, the cycle of boom and bust may have begun anew, as the market had already erased nearly half of recent losses by the end of 2009.

To think about how older workers might react to stock market fluctuations, we reframe the market movements shown in figure 4-1 in terms of how the rate of return on stock market investments has changed over time. This allows us to compare recent and historical returns. To calculate the annual rate of return, we use the percent change in the monthly average S&P 500 from one December to the next, as general perceptions about whether the market has had a good or bad year are based on returns over the calendar year. In making this calculation, we remove the effect of inflation, so subsequent figures show the real return on stock assets. To see why this is important, suppose the stock market went up by 10 percent over the year and inflation was also 10 percent. In such a case, the increase in the market is just sufficient to ensure that the stocks held by the investor provide the same purchasing power at year's end as they did at the beginning of the year. The investor has earned no real return on his or her investment in this year.

The actual pattern over the past thirty years is one of tremendous year-to-year volatility (see figure 4-2). In the 1980s and early 1990s, there often would be two good years with 10 to 20 percent real returns, followed by a bad year with zero or even negative returns. Since then, the market has experienced more prolonged booms and busts, including two five-year rallies in the late 1990s and mid-2000s, as well as a multiyear bear market in the early 2000s. The real annual return in 2008 was negative 40 percent, by far the worst one-year return in recent history.

Not surprisingly, these dramatic turnarounds in equity markets have captured the public's attention. The question at hand, though, is whether they alter retirement decisions. Given that there has always been substantial year-to-year variability in stock prices, as indicated by the frequent switching between years of positive and negative returns,

Figure 4-2. *Annual Real Return in S&P 500 Index, 1979–2009*

Annual percent change

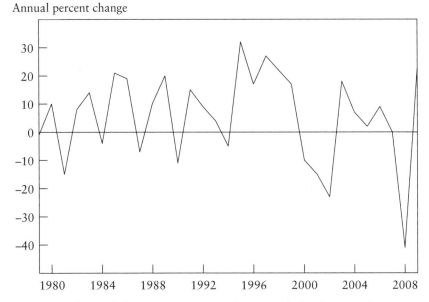

Source: Authors' calculations using S&P 500 data (www.freelunch.com) and consumer price index data (www.bls.gov). Annual returns calculated using December monthly average.

is it sensible to expect a single year's market performance—even a very bad year—to drive behavior?

Ultimately this is an empirical question, and one we test later in the chapter. But it seems possible that the market return over a longer period of time could play a more important role in retirement decisions. If workers understand that a bad year in the market could easily be followed by a good year that may make up for much or all of their losses, then a single bad year in the market may have little effect on their retirement behavior. If, however, workers experience weak returns over a longer period of time—say, five or ten years—their ability to wait out the bear market may be diminished.

When the real return in the S&P 500 Index is calculated over five and ten years, the average five-year return in the past thirty years is 32 percent, while the average ten-year return is 65 percent (figure 4-3). This

Figure 4-3. *Five-Year and Ten-Year Real Return in S&P 500 Index, 1979–2009*

Percent change

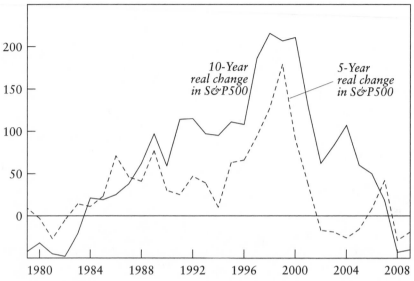

Source: Authors' calculations using S&P 500 data (www.freelunch.com) and consumer price index data (www.bk.gov). Annual returns calculated using December monthly average.

is roughly equivalent to earning a 5 percent real return a year, once the effect of compounding is taken into account. There is clearly substantial variability over time in these longer-term returns as well. In the 1980s and early 1990s, the five-year real return was generally about 50 percent. Subsequently, real returns rose, hitting almost 200 percent in the year 2000 before collapsing to small or even negative values. Ten-year returns are somewhat higher, as expected, but the patterns are similar.

These statistics suggest that market returns could have a significant impact on retirement behavior. A worker approaching retirement age could have tripled the value of his portfolio over a five-year period, while another worker could have seen his portfolio remain constant or even shrink. If workers have considerable resources invested in the stock market, a boom or a bust in the period leading up to traditional retirement ages could play a key role in the decision of when to retire. The question is, do older workers have enough stock assets for this to be the case?

Stock Holdings of Older Workers

Even the dramatic rises and falls in the stock market depicted in figure 4-1 will not affect overall retirement rates in any meaningful way if relatively few people own stocks or if typical stock holdings are very small. In assessing the stock holdings of workers now nearing retirement age, it is also important to compare the holdings of different demographic groups, such as those with high and low levels of education, since our empirical approach (discussed subsequently) is to compare how groups with more and less stock market exposure respond to market fluctuations.

The primary source of wealth data in the United States is the Survey of Consumer Finances (SCF). The survey has been conducted every three years since 1983, most recently in 2007, with a sample of roughly 4,500 households per survey. Since U.S. wealth tends to be fairly concentrated, the SCF oversamples households of high net worth in order to obtain a more accurate estimate of total national wealth holdings. It collects detailed data on respondents' assets and income, including balances in retirement accounts such as 401(k)s and information on how they are invested. We draw on the 2007 SCF for information on the stock holdings of households nearing retirement age at the time of the recent market decline. Because the SCF oversamples households of high net worth, we use sample weights to obtain statistics that are representative of the general population.

Table 4-1 shows stock holdings in the 2007 SCF, just as stock assets were peaking before the most recent market decline. The households here are headed by individuals between the ages of fifty-five and sixty-four, the age group in which workers are likely to be contemplating retirement. We examine several types of stock holdings: directly held stocks, stock-based mutual funds held outside of retirement accounts,

Table 4-1. *Stock Holdings of Households Aged Fifty-Five to Sixty-Four, by Education Group, 2007*

Category	Percent with stock holdings	Median value conditional on holding	Value of holdings, all households, by percentile					
			25th	50th	75th	90th	95th	99th
All								
Directly held stocks	21.3	24,000	0	0	0	25,000	125,000	1,000,000
Stock mutual funds (nonretirement)	14.0	97,000	0	0	0	45,000	191,000	1,130,000
Stocks in retirement accounts	50.0	66,500	0	20	66,500	230,000	447,500	1,174,050
Any stocks	58.3	78,000	0	8,000	97,500	357,620	752,000	3,065,000
Less than high school								
Directly held stocks	5.4	270	0	0	0	0	50	28,000
Stock mutual funds (nonretirement)	1.9	3,000	0	0	0	0	0	3,000
Stocks in retirement accounts	21.4	10,000	0	0	0	10,000	70,000	325,000
Any stocks	21.4	10,000	0	0	0	10,000	70,000	353,000

High school								
Directly held stocks	12.7	9,000	0	0	0	500	14,000	97,000
Stock mutual funds (nonretirement)	6.9	50,000	0	0	0	0	38,000	250,000
Stocks in retirement accounts	36.6	33,800	0	0	15,000	88,000	188,800	455,000
Any stocks	46.0	35,000	0	0	28,500	130,000	212,500	560,000
Some college								
Directly held stocks	15.6	3,500	0	0	0	2,000	15,000	342,000
Stock mutual funds (non-retirement)	6.0	45,000	0	0	0	0	20,000	300,000
Stocks in retirement accounts	50.3	60,000	0	20	61,600	160,000	224,000	590,000
Any stocks	55.8	65,000	0	4,000	73,500	197,150	319,500	603,000
College graduate								
Directly held stocks	34.2	60,000	0	0	13,000	154,000	500,000	2,100,000
Stock mutual funds (nonretirement)	26.0	107,000	0	0	4,700	200,000	385,000	3,000,000
Stocks in retirement accounts	66.8	85,000	0	27,000	159,600	480,000	775,800	2,330,000
Any stocks	77.5	125,000	3,250	65,100	271,300	846,000	1,865,000	6,022,500

Source: Survey of Consumer Finances. Data are weighted to be representative of the U.S. population.

and stocks held inside retirement accounts, including both 401(k)-type pension plans and individual retirement accounts (IRAs).

Though far from universal, stock ownership in this age group is fairly common: more than half (58 percent) of the households own stocks. The most common form of stock ownership is through retirement accounts (50 percent of households in this group), though some households own stocks directly (21 percent) or in stock-based mutual funds outside of retirement accounts (14 percent). Although this level of ownership is reasonably high, the typical older household's stock holdings are quite small. The median value (50th percentile) of all stock assets among households owning any stocks is $78,000, but the median value across all households, including those that do not own stocks, is just $8,000. Fewer than 25 percent of older households have $100,000 or more in stock assets. While it is hard to quantify the threshold level of stock assets above which stock fluctuations should matter for retirement—a subject we return to later in the chapter—it is clear from table 4-1 that the number of households with large stock holdings is relatively small.

When levels of stock holdings are assessed by level of education, striking differences emerge, again shown in table 4-1. The share of households with any stock-based investments is 21 percent for high school dropouts and 46 percent for high school graduates versus 78 percent for college graduates. Among households that own stock, the typical level of all stock assets is $35,000 for high school graduates and $125,000 for college graduates. Among all households headed by a high school graduate, including households with no assets, those at the 75th percentile (where 75 percent of households have fewer assets than this household and 25 percent have more) has just $28,500 in stock assets. For households headed by a college graduate, the corresponding figure is $271,300. In short, college graduates have a much higher degree of participation in the stock market than do high school graduates and dropouts.

Although the typical household approaching retirement in 2007 had relatively small stock holdings, this likely represents an increase compared with the stock holdings of earlier cohorts. Estimates for earlier years are complicated by the fact that some previous SCF surveys did not ask about the asset allocation in all relevant accounts. Using other data, we can nonetheless infer that equity holdings have risen dramatically over time. Table 4-1 suggests that the vast majority of stock-based investments for most households are stocks held in retirement accounts, and participation in these accounts has increased markedly over time. According to the Employee Benefit Research Institute (2009), for example, the share of pension plan participants at medium and large firms that had a defined contribution (or 401(k)-type) plan rose from 34 percent in 1980 to 64 percent in 2005. In all likelihood, stock holdings were much lower when many fewer households held such accounts and those that did had only recently established them.[1]

Note, however, that quantifying the level of stock assets held by older households as they approach retirement does not directly convey the effect of a sharp market decline on households' future retirement income. To fill this gap, we examine different levels of stock holdings ranging from none to $500,000 and identify the fraction of households headed by an individual between ages fifty-five and sixty-four that have stock holdings at that level or lower (table 4-2). About 42 percent have no holdings at all, 75 percent have $100,000 or less, and 92 percent have $500,000 or less, leaving only 8 percent with stock holdings above this level. We then compute the loss that would be experienced by households at each stock threshold if their portfolios fell by 50 percent—which is the same distance the S&P 500 fell in the recent market decline, though it has since made up for some of those losses. To approximate the drop in annual retirement income that would result from the market crash, we make the simplifying assumption that households will consume 5 percent of their wealth a year during retirement, and we divide this by 12 to get the drop in monthly income.

1. Despite the growing importance of defined contribution plans, Gustman, Steinmeier, and Tabatabai (2010) provide evidence that defined benefit plans still play a more important role for those currently nearing retirement age. For more details on these two types of plans, see chapter 2 of this volume.

Table 4-2. *Stock Losses of Households Aged Fifty-Five to Sixty-Four in 2008 Market Crash, Dollars*[a]

Stock assets in 2007 SCF	Percent of sample w/assets at/below	Asset loss	Lost retirement income	
			Annual	Monthly
0	41.7	0	0	0
25,000	58.7	12,500	625	52
50,000	65.4	25,000	1,250	104
100,000	75.1	50,000	2,500	208
250,000	86.9	125,000	6,250	521
500,000	92.0	250,000	12,500	1,042

a. Calculations are based on stock holdings of households aged fifty-five to sixty-four based on data from the 2007 Survey of Consumer of Finances. Calculations assume a 50 percent decline in assets from 2007 value. Lost retirement income is calculated by assuming that household will consume 5 percent of wealth each year.

It appears that if households spread the losses due to a steep market decline evenly over their retirement years, the drop in retirement income would be modest for most of them. For example, those with $100,000 of equity holdings would lose $2,500 a year, or $208 a month, as a result of the stock market crash. These are not insignificant numbers, but they are likely to be small in relation to the household's retirement income. Obviously, the losses would be even smaller for those with less than $100,000 invested in stocks, a group that includes 75 percent of older households in 2007.

Hence, few older households lost enough money in the recent stock market crash to experience a substantial drop in their future retirement income.[2] This would suggest that the effect of the market crash on overall retirement rates would be small, as few households would have lost

2. Gustman, Steinmeier, and Tabatabai (2009) come to a similar conclusion using even more detailed wealth data (including Social Security and pension wealth) available in the Health and Retirement Survey. They found the share of wealth associated with stocks to be so small that even a dramatic decline in the stock market is unlikely to have retirement implications for many workers.

enough income to induce them to work longer to make up for the loss. Nonetheless, one can envision scenarios under which the retirement response would be greater. Suppose individuals planned to use their stock assets to finance a few years of consumption between the time they retire and the time they start collecting Social Security benefits, rather than spreading them out over the full length of their retirement. In this case, even small losses in stock holdings—such as those experienced by most households—could lead workers to delay retirement, if for just a short period, and this would generate a larger overall effect on retirement.

In the end, whether the stock market crash of 2008 led to a significant change in retirement behavior is an empirical question. Since the crash is still very recent as of this writing, one way to gauge its effect is to look at the effect of past market fluctuations on retirement behavior and use the resulting estimates to predict the effect of the 2008 decline. The appeal of this approach goes beyond the simple fact that it can be implemented now, before all the recent data on post-crash labor market behavior become available. The most plausible alternative approach— that of simply looking at the change in retirement rates between 2007 and 2008 and inferring that the difference is the effect of the market crash—fails to take into account that other things may also have changed during this time period, so the observed change in retirement rates may not accurately reflect the true effect of the market decline (recall figure 3-1, which points to important trends in retirement behavior over time). To identify the effect of market fluctuations on retirement, it is essential to control for other factors.

Empirical Analysis

In attempting to mimic a controlled experiment, we take into account the ups and downs of the stock market over time, noting that some individuals are exposed to unusually strong or weak stock market conditions near the time of retirement (the "treatment group") whereas others are exposed to more normal market conditions (the "control group").[3] If we compare the average retirement rate in the two groups, controlling for individual-specific factors such as age and education that could also influence retirement decisions and for any long-run trends in retirement behavior over time (such as those evident in figure 3-1), the difference should reflect the effect of the unusual market conditions.

One can construct an even stronger test of the effect of the stock market on retirement by noting that different individuals are more or less affected by stock market fluctuations by virtue of having greater or lesser stock holdings. Although the Current Population Survey (CPS) provides weak data on stock holdings, the fact that stock holdings vary strongly with education level (see table 4-1) enables us to treat education as a sort of proxy for stock ownership. The question then is whether more highly educated households are more sensitive to stock market fluctuations than less educated households when making retirement decisions. That is, are the former households more likely to retire early when the market performs well and late when the market performs badly? If this is the case, it would provide even stronger evidence that the stock market affects retirement decisions.

The next step is to decide what measure of stock market returns to use in the analysis. As mentioned, the S&P 500 is our preferred measure of the value of the stock market, but over what time period should we calculate changes in this index? The answer is that the right measure of stock market returns is the one workers respond to in making decisions, and this is something we cannot know until we conduct the analysis. Therefore, we estimate our models using the one-year, five-year, and ten-year real return in the S&P 500 in order to test which measure of returns (if any) has the biggest effect on workers' retirement decisions.

We first estimate how workers' retirement decisions would respond to a 25 percentage point increase in the one-year rate of return in the stock

---

3. A more technical discussion of our methods and results is available in Coile and Levine (2009).

Figure 4-4. *Effect of Rising Stock Market on Retirement Rates, by Age and Education*[a]

Percent change in retirement rates

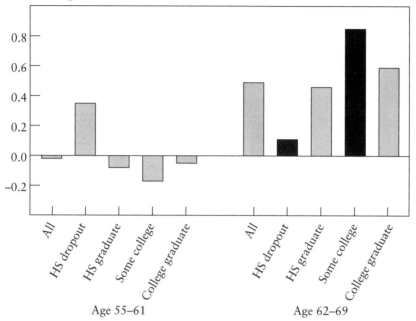

Age 55–61   Age 62–69

Source: Authors' calculations from Current Population Surveys.
a. Twenty-five-point increase in one-year real return. Statistically significant results are shaded in black, and insignificant results in gray.

market (see figure 4-4). This would mean, for example, a return that goes up from an average value of 5 percent to 30 percent. Then we examine the impact of a 100 percentage point increase in the ten-year rate of return (figure 4-5). We also calculated five-year rates of return but for brevity omit them since they are qualitatively similar to our estimates for the ten-year rate of return. The increases in the one-year and ten-year returns we have chosen to examine (25-point and 100-point, respectively) are designed to simulate the impact of a large, yet plausible, change in stock prices.[4] The two figures show the differential responsiveness by

4. Over the past three decades, the standard deviation in one-year and ten-year market returns is 16 percent and 78 percent, respectively.

Figure 4-5. *Effect of Rising Stock Market on Retirement Rates, by Age and Education*[a]

Percent change in retirement rates

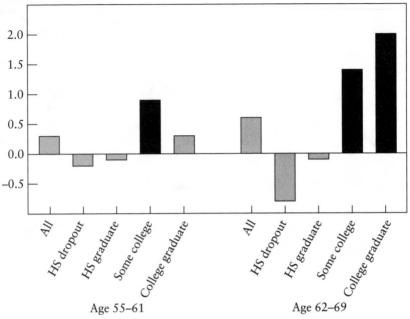

Age 55–61   Age 62–69

Source: Authors' calculations from Current Population Surveys.
a. Hundred-point increase in ten-year real return. Statistically significant results are shaded in black and insignificant results in gray.

workers' age and level of education to the one-year and ten-year market increases. We focus mainly on estimates that are statistically different from zero.

We find little evidence in these results that the younger group of workers (fifty-five to sixty-one) respond to large market increases by retiring sooner. The estimated impact is small, mainly statistically insignificant, and inconsistent across educational attainment categories.

Workers between the ages of sixty-two and sixty-nine, however, do appear to alter their retirement decisions. The evidence that workers in this age group respond to longer-term movements in the stock market is reasonably strong. The pattern across educational attainment categories is exactly what we predicted: no statistically significant impact on retirement for less educated workers, but larger and statistically significant increases in retirement for more educated ones. In terms of magnitude, a 100-point increase in the ten-year return raises the probability of retirement by 1.4 points for those with some college and 2.0 points for college graduates. This is an increase of 10 and 17 percent, respectively, compared with each group's baseline retirement rate.

For short-term rates of return, the evidence is weaker. Although we find a positive relationship between market returns and retirement rates among high school graduates and the college-educated, the gradient associated with education is less clear. The peak responsiveness is estimated to occur for those who began, but did not complete, their college education. Those with a college degree are found to respond in much the same way as those with a high school degree. It is possible that our statistical methods are not sufficient to delineate more clearly these differential impacts across educational attainment groups. All the same, our current evidence discourages strong conclusions regarding the impact of short-term market fluctuations on retirement, even among workers sixty-two to sixty-nine.

In sum, we find some empirical evidence that workers alter their retirement behavior in response to stock market fluctuations, delaying retirement when market returns are low and retiring early when the market performs better than expected. This effect is clearly strongest for those who have more education and are between the ages of sixty-two and sixty-nine. The stronger effect for those with more education is exactly what we expect to find on the basis of the higher level of stock holdings for this group. The greater responsiveness after age sixty-two is also not surprising, since more workers in this age group are seriously contemplating retirement; access to Social Security benefits also may play a role. Not surprisingly, older workers respond to long-term rather than short-term changes in stock market fluctuations; as figure 4-1 showed, one year's gains or losses are often erased the following year.

Summary and Conclusions

At first glance, the recent stock market crash seemed to have the potential to substantially alter retirement decisions. By historical standards, the 40 percent decline in the market in 2008 is its worst one-year performance in recent times, though the market had erased half of those losses by the end of 2009. Perhaps more significant, the five-year and ten-year returns for the periods ending in 2008 and 2009 are as bad as those experienced in the early 1980s, following a disastrous decade for the market.

Yet the effects of even this very bad period in the stock market on retirement behavior may be mitigated by the fact that the typical household approaching retirement has very little in the way of stock assets. While the shift toward defined contribution pension plans has certainly raised the number of households with stock assets, typical values in those accounts are still low for the households now reaching retirement age. As a result, the losses in future retirement income that these households will experience because of the recent market decline are likely to be small. In general, only highly educated workers have a large amount of stock assets, so they are the only ones likely to be much affected by the market decline.

Empirically, we find only limited evidence that workers respond to market fluctuations in making retirement decisions. Although older workers (aged sixty-two to sixty-nine) with more education appear to respond to long-term market movements, younger workers and those with less education do not. Evidence that workers respond to short-term market movements is considerably weaker.

Thus, some workers may delay retirement as a result of the recent stock market decline, although most will be more highly educated workers. Next, we turn to our analysis of the housing and labor markets before reporting estimates of the numbers of workers affected by each market downturn.

5 | *Impact of the Housing Market Crash*

Although the origins of the current economic crisis will surely be debated for years to come, most analysts agree that risky lending in the housing market contributed to the crisis by helping to create a bubble in housing prices and leaving banks in a precarious position when the bubble burst. Plunging house prices put millions of Americans "under water" on their homes, owing more on them than they are worth at present. Older households are less likely to be in this position, many having purchased their homes long ago, but they are not immune to the consequences of the housing market collapse. Older homeowners who had planned to sell their homes and use some of the proceeds to help finance their retirement will now have less equity for that purpose because of lower housing prices. In areas that have experienced a rash of foreclosures, older homeowners may find themselves unable to sell their homes altogether, at least in the short term. Like a drop in stock market wealth, declines in home equity may lead households to delay retirement.

We explore the possible effects in much the same way as we did for the stock market crash. First, we examine the magnitude of the recent plunge in house prices, to see how deep and rare this drop is by historical standards. Second, we look at levels of home ownership and home equity among households nearing retirement age, as we would expect the recent decline in house prices to have a significant effect on retirement decisions only if people have a substantial amount of home equity. Third, we conduct an empirical analysis to assess whether there is a causal link between house price fluctuations and retirement behavior.

Again we draw on thirty years of data from the Current Population Survey (CPS), this time taking into account the fact that different geographic areas experience different house price movements over time. In the empirical approach, we examine how retirement decisions made in places and at times where prices are rapidly rising or falling compare to those made in places and at times when prices are flat. We refine this test further by comparing the effects of house price movements on the behavior of homeowners and renters. If an increase in house prices raises the probability that homeowners—but not renters—retire, this would be compelling evidence that house price movements do affect retirement behavior.

Housing Market Fluctuations

To get a sense of the significance of the recent decline in relation to past price fluctuations, we rely on two consistent measures of housing prices. Each is constructed slightly differently, with its own advantages and disadvantages.

The first measure is the Standard and Poor's Case-Shiller Home Price Index (CS). This index, instituted in 1987 for fourteen metropolitan areas, has now been expanded to twenty areas. Calculated on a monthly basis, the index covers very large cities such as New York, Los Angeles, and Chicago, as well as cities with populations close to 400,000, such as Cleveland, Minneapolis, and Tampa. Through a "repeat sales pricing" method, the CS index collects data on sale prices of individual single-family homes from county records and matches them to each home's previous sales price; then the change in sales prices of these homes is aggregated to create the index. Trends in national home prices can be ascertained from composite indices based on either ten or twenty metro areas, the latter available only since 2000. For our purposes, we rely on the ten-area composite index in our discussion of national house price movements.[1]

Our second source of data on house price movements is the Office of Federal Housing Enterprise Oversight Home Price Index (OFHEO). This index has been calculated quarterly at the state level since 1975, and a national version is available as well. Like the CS index, the OFHEO index is based on repeat sales price changes in the value of individual homes over time, but it is calculated using data on mortgages originated by Fannie Mae and Freddie Mac during home purchase and refinancing transactions. These mortgages are directed toward lower- and moderate-income families that are for the most part purchasing lower-priced homes.

Unlike the CS index, the OFHEO index is available for all states and years, which is convenient for empirical analysis because it can be used to assign each person in our CPS sample a measure of house price changes. The CS index provides no measure of house price changes for anyone outside the twenty metro areas or in any period before 1987 so it can only be applied to a portion of the available CPS data. On the other hand, the CS index exhibits more dramatic changes over time as it includes both foreclosures and more expensive houses, whereas the OFHEO index focuses on more moderately priced homes. Which index is preferable remains unclear, leading us to use both in our analysis.

In examining house price changes, we are interested not in the level of the index per se but rather in how it changes over time (see figure 5-1). Both indices are set so that they take on the value of 100 in the year 2000. We have used the consumer price index to convert all price changes from that level to real values, so the change in the indices can be interpreted as the change in real house prices, net of inflation.

With the OFHEO index, we find some ups and downs in real house prices from the mid-1970s through early 1990s, but their magnitude is only on the order of 10 percent (10 points on the index scale) from a

1. The ten metro areas included in the index are Boston, Chicago, Denver, Las Vegas, Los Angeles, Miami, New York City, San Diego, San Francisco, and Washington, D.C.

Figure 5-1. *OFHEO and Case-Shiller Home Price Index*[a]

OFHEO Index (year 2000 = 100)

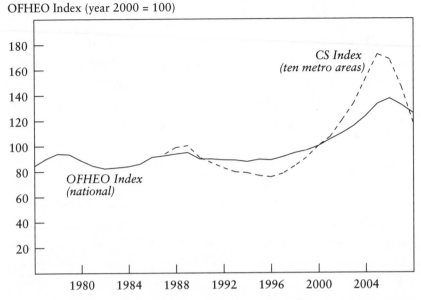

a. Indices converted to real values using the consumer price index.

peak to a trough, or vice versa. By the end of this twenty-year period, real home prices had barely increased at all. By contrast, between 1994 and 2006 real house prices rose more than 50 percent (from 87 to 137 in the index), before falling 9 percent by 2008 (a 12 index-point decline on a base of 137).

Since initiated in 1987, the CS index for ten metro areas has shown a similar but somewhat more extreme pattern. Whereas the OFHEO index was flat during the early 1990s, the real CS index fell by nearly 25 percent between 1989 and 1996. Between 1996 and 2005, the real CS index rose more than 125 percent (compared with 50 percent for the OFHEO index), then fell by one-third between 2005 and 2008 (compared with 9 percent for the OFHEO index for a similar period). As noted earlier, these differences can be attributed to differences in the construction of the two indices, such as the fact that the CS index includes foreclosures, covers only ten metro areas (some of which, like

Figure 5-2. *Annual Percentage Change in Real House Prices*

Percent change

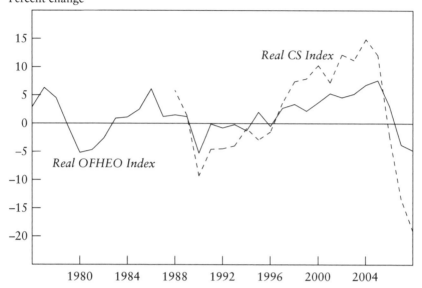

Las Vegas, experienced a particularly extreme boom-and-bust cycle), and includes some more expensive houses. Despite differences in the magnitude of these swings, the patterns over time follow a very similar track in the two indices.

When we recast the house price movements shown in figure 5-1 in terms of how the rate of return on housing investments has changed over time, we found that the annual real rate of return for the national OFHEO index and ten-area CS index follow a similar pattern as well, but the magnitude of the changes is larger in the CS index (figure 5-2). While the annual return during the boom period of the mid-1990s to the mid-2000s is generally on the order of 5 percent in the OFHEO data and never tops 7 percent, real annual increases are more like 10 percent in the CS data and reach as high as 15 percent in one year. Conversely, the CS index falls by 15 to 20 percent a year in both 2007 and 2008, as opposed to 4 to 5 percent a year for the OFHEO index.

Their differences aside, the similarities between these indices are of considerable interest. Both show weak returns in the early 1990s, followed by an unusually long period of sustained strong returns in the late 1990s and early 2000s. Returns in 2007 and 2008 were very poor by any measure—for the CS index, they were the worst in its twenty-year history, while for the OFHEO index they were rivaled only by the housing bust of the early 1980s.

In assessing whether workers will change their retirement behavior following an unusually large rise or fall in house prices, one must take into account the fact that the recent housing boom and bust played out over the course of many years; thus it is likely to be the cumulative effect of several years of good (or bad) returns rather than a single year's return that influences behavior. To elaborate, consider the real return in the OFHEO and CS indices calculated over a five-year period (figure 5-3) rather than a one-year period, as before. Although once again the returns are more extreme with the CS index, the key observation from both series is that workers reaching retirement age at different points in time will have experienced radically different returns on their housing investments in the run-up to retirement. According to the CS index, a worker reaching his early sixties in 1994, for example, will have experienced a 20 percent real loss in housing wealth over the preceding five years, whereas a worker reaching that age ten years later will have experienced a 70 percent real gain. If workers have a substantial amount of home equity and base their retirement decisions in part on changes in the value of that home equity, these types of differences have the potential to change people's behavior.

So far we have concentrated on national data (or a composite of ten metro areas, in the case of the CS index). But housing markets are local, so workers should respond to the movement of house prices in their local housing market rather than in the country as a whole. This means that workers will experience different house price returns not only because of differences in the year that they reach retirement age (as discussed with regard to figure 5-3), but also because of differences in where they live. Thus it becomes easier to identify the effect of house

Figure 5-3. *Five-Year Percentage Change in Real House Prices*

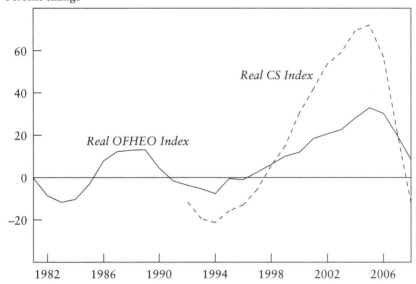

Percent change

price movements on retirement, if indeed such an effect exists, while controlling for any time trends that might affect the retirement behavior of workers everywhere.

In figure 5-4, we use CS data to plot house price returns over time in a few metropolitan areas selected to illustrate the wide-ranging experiences of different geographic areas. One of these areas is Los Angeles, which experienced two housing booms during the time period for which CS data are available: a smaller one in the late 1980s and a larger one in the mid-1990s through the mid-2000s. The second boom was much larger in Los Angeles than in most other cities, with real house prices rising by nearly 200 percent over a single decade. By contrast, Cleveland did not experience any significant boom or bust during this period. Rather, prices grew very slowly over nearly the entire period, falling slightly at the very end. The experience of Boston provides an intermediate case. Both of Boston's housing booms were smaller and came to an end earlier than the booms in Los Angeles. In the case of the more

Figure 5-4. *Case-Shiller Home Price Index in Selected Metro Areas*[a]

CS Index (January 2000 = 100)

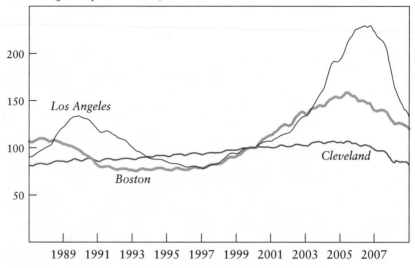

1989 1991 1993 1995 1997 1999 2001 2003 2005 2007

a. Indices are converted to real values using the consumer price index.

recent boom, prices rose by only half as much as in Los Angeles and began to slide nearly a year and a half earlier. To reiterate, the fact that workers' experiences vary so dramatically across geographic areas will help to identify the effect of house price fluctuations on retirement.

Home Equity Holdings of Older Workers

In the next step of our analysis we return to the 2007 Survey of Consumer Finances (SCF; see chapter 4), this time to measure workers' home equity holdings (net of mortgages or any other debt) and determine whether they are substantial enough to affect retirement behavior during fluctuations in house prices. Among households headed by those between the ages of fifty-five and sixty-four, fully 81 percent own their own homes (table 5-1). The gradient with respect to education is not terribly steep: although the ownership rate is only 64 percent for high school dropouts, it is fairly similar for the other three education groups.

Table 5-1. *Home Equity Holdings of Households Aged Fifty-Five to Sixty-Four, by Education Group, 2007*

Category	All	Less than high school	High school	Some college	College graduate
Percent with holdings	81	64	81	80	86
Median dollar value conditional on holding	140,000	64,000	116,000	130,000	201,000
Dollar value of holdings, all households, by percentile					
25th	21,000	0	13,000	22,000	58,000
50th	100,000	24,000	78,000	93,000	160,000
75th	231,000	73,000	170,000	200,000	355,000
90th	420,000	135,400	274,000	369,000	600,000
95th	600,000	225,000	345,000	490,000	985,000
99th	1,500,000	300,000	582,000	800,000	2,030,000

Source: Survey of Consumer Finances. Data are weighted to be representative of the U.S. population.

Levels of home equity are also fairly high for this age group. The typical (median) value of home equity for all the homeowners is $140,000. This amount varies to a certain extent with level of education, but the relationship between asset holdings and education is not nearly as strong as it was for stocks. When all households (including non-homeowners) with a high school education are ranked in order of the amount of their home equity, the household at the 75th percentile (where 75 percent of households have lower home equity and 25 percent have more) has $170,000 in home equity. Among college graduates, the equivalent figure is $355,000.

Notably, the difference between the holdings of college graduates versus those of high school graduates is on the order of 2 to 1, whereas it was nearly 10 to 1 for stocks. Furthermore, $170,000 is a fairly large sum of money; the comparable figure for stock holdings was only $28,500. With home equity values at this level, if one household sees its home equity double during the five-year period leading up to retirement while another sees it fall by half, it seems plausible that workers in these two families might make different retirement decisions. Inasmuch as households, including less-educated ones, hold home equity more broadly than stock assets, many could be affected if house prices turn sharply higher or lower.

To estimate the level of home equity losses experienced by households in the recent housing market bust, we simulated a 33 percent drop in real home values, which is the actual drop experienced in the CS composite index between 2006 and 2008. Of course, losses may have been bigger or smaller in individual housing markets—according to the CS data, the housing market dropped as much as 50 percent in some areas (Phoenix, Las Vegas), but only 10 to 15 percent in others (Charlotte, Dallas, Denver). The real drop in the national OFHEO index over this period was smaller, on the order of 12 percent. Thus a 33 percent drop may be taken to reflect the actual experience of certain metro areas but to be somewhat larger than the average national effect.

We simulated the impact of this drop for households that have between $0 and $500,000 in home equity holdings (table 5-2). We find roughly one in five (19 percent) have no home equity, and about half (49 percent) have less than $100,000 (including those households with none).[2] When these figures are compared with the stock assets in table 4-2, households are shown to have more home equity than stock assets. Whereas 75 percent of households have less than $100,000 in stocks, for example, the same proportion have less than $250,000 in home equity. At the same time, the share of households with very large amounts ($500,000 or more) of either type of asset is only about 8 percent (92 percent have less than $500,000).

Table 5-2 also shows the estimated loss in annual or monthly income after a 33 percent drop in housing values if households had planned to consume 5 percent of their home equity each year. By construction, the

2. Because the fall in the housing market began in 2006, our calculations may slightly underestimate actual losses suffered in the crash, since the values reported in the 2007 SCF may be lower than housing values at the peak of the market. Nonetheless, there is enough uncertainty in our simple calculations—for example, as to whether 33 percent is the right drop in housing market values to use—that this is not likely to be an important issue.

Table 5-2. *Hypothetical Home Equity Losses of Households Aged Fifty-Five to Sixty-Four in Recent Housing Market Crash, Dollars*[a]

Home equity in 2007 SCF	Percent of sample w/ equity at/below	Equity loss	Lost retirement income	
			Annual	Monthly
0	19.2	0	0	0
25,000	25.2	8,250	413	34
50,000	30.9	16,500	825	69
100,000	48.9	33,000	1,650	138
250,000	76.0	82,500	4,125	344
500,000	91.7	165,000	8,250	688

a. Calculations are based on home equity holdings of households aged fifty-five to sixty-four in the 2007 Survey of Consumer of Finances. Calculations assume a 33 percent decline in assets from 2007 value. Lost retirement income is calculated by assuming that household will consume 5 percent of home equity each year.

lost income amounts at each threshold level are smaller than those in table 4-2, where we simulated a 50 percent drop in stock assets. Nonetheless, because home equity holdings are larger than stock holdings, typical income losses resulting from the housing market crash may be larger than those from the stock market crash. Our simple calculation suggests that 75 percent of households would have experienced a monthly retirement income loss of $344 or less when the housing market fell, compared with a loss of $208 or less when the stock market crashed.

Our calculations suggest that the lost wealth and available retirement income associated with the collapse in the housing market are at least as large as that associated with the collapse of the stock market. If workers respond to housing price movements in making retirement decisions, it may be reasonable to expect a larger response in the face of the collapse in the housing market. We now test this proposition formally.

Empirical Analysis

As in chapter 4, we use thirty years of CPS data to assess the relationship between house price movements and retirement behavior. The key variable of interest is the real return on housing investments. Since the period for which this should be calculated is not obvious, we use both the one-year and five-year return. In calculating house price returns, we use both the CS and OFHEO indices and estimate our models separately with each return measure in order to see if our results are sensitive to the choice of housing index.

As mentioned earlier, this exercise differs from our analysis of stock market fluctuations in that house price returns vary not only over time but also across geographic areas. This makes it easier to identify their effect on retirement while still controlling for any time-specific factors that affect all locations (such as a tendency of workers to retire later in our sample period owing to changes in Social Security or private pensions) or for location-specific factors that do not change over time (such as a tendency of workers in state X to retire earlier than those in state Y). Furthermore, data on whether individuals are homeowners or renters enable us to refine our test in that we expect homeowners to be more responsive to house price fluctuations than renters, since only homeowners experience a positive or negative wealth shock when house prices go up or down.[3] Evidence to this effect would be strongly suggestive of a causal link between housing prices and retirement.

When we examine the one-year return to housing investments, we find no evidence of a significant effect on retirement, nor of a stronger response by homeowners. This is perhaps not too surprising, as it is more likely to take several years of good or bad returns to affect behavior.

We then repeat this exercise using the five-year return. Specifically, we project the impact of a 34 percentage point increase in the five-year return on housing investments using the CS index, and a 13 percentage point increase using the OFHEO index (see figure 5-5). We chose these different values for the two indices because they reflect the standard deviation

---

3. Arguably, renters may be worse off when house prices go up, as they can expect their rent to go up as well. However, this would only strengthen our expectation that the probability of homeowners retiring when house prices go up would increase in relation to the response of renters.

Figure 5-5. *Effect of Rising Housing Prices on Retirement Rates*[a]

Percent change in retirement rates

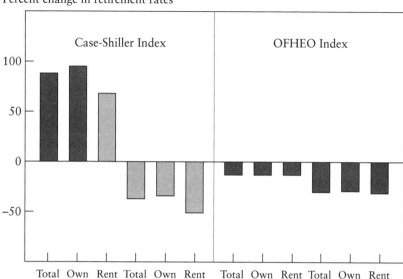

Source: Authors' calculations from Current Population Surveys.
a. Increase in Five-Year Real Return. Bars show effect of a one standard deviation increase in returns. This reflects a 34 percentage point increase in returns in the Case-Shiller index and a 12 percentage point increase in the OFHEO index.

in returns over time. Thus our simulations model the impact of an increase in housing prices that is a full standard deviation in each index.

The results for workers aged fifty-five to sixty-one on the CS index show some indication of the expected effect. A 34-point increase in the five-year return on housing investments (which would be the equivalent of moving from a typical five-year real return of 20 percent to a very strong return of 54 percent) increases the probability of retirement by a statistically significant 0.88 percentage points, or 18 percent compared with the average retirement rate.

Although this initial finding seems consistent with the hypothesis that retirement rates rise with housing prices, little else in our analysis supports it. First, the impact of price changes for homeowners is only somewhat larger than that observed for renters. The fact that the two estimates are not statistically different suggests that factors other than changes in home prices may be the cause of the change in retirement behavior.

Another issue is that our estimates do not indicate the expected stronger response for older workers, who are closer to retirement and should be more sensitive to house price movements than younger workers. A 10 percent rise in assets, for example, might be enough to allow a worker one year away from the planned retirement date to retire immediately, whereas a worker who is still five years away will be unaffected, at least in the short term. The fact that workers aged sixty-two and older have access to Social Security (and in some cases pension) benefits might also make them more responsive to market fluctuations. Moreover, the estimated impact of stock prices (chapter 4) and of labor market conditions (chapter 6) on retirement are consistent with our intuition that older workers are more responsive.

In summary, when we use the CS index, we find no evidence that workers aged sixty-two to sixty-nine are more likely to retire when housing prices rise. Nor are there signs of a stronger response from homeowners than from renters in this age group. For both groups, higher housing returns appear to lower the probability of retirement, though the effects are not significant.

When we use the OFHEO index to measure changes in house prices, we find no indication that higher returns in the housing market alter retirement behavior. Every coefficient estimated in these models, for workers at different ages and for owners and renters alike, is wrong-signed (and even statistically significant). Rather, they suggest that rising house prices lead to fewer retirements. We can only conclude that some other spurious factor is linked to housing prices, and that rising prices, with their higher returns on housing investment, do not in themselves bring about earlier retirement.

Summary and Conclusions

At first glance, the suggestion that workers responded to home equity losses associated with the recent housing market crash by retiring later seems quite plausible. House price movements—particularly those experienced during the boom-and-bust cycle of the mid-1990s to the late 2000s—were sufficiently large to have a potential effect on retirement behavior. One household might see its real housing wealth double over a five-year period, while another household reaching retirement age at a different point in time or living in a different geographic area might see its housing wealth cut in half. It is reasonable to think that these two households might make different retirement decisions as a result of their differing experiences in the housing market. Furthermore, home equity is more broadly held than stock assets and the level of home equity holdings is often fairly substantial, making it still more likely that workers respond to large price fluctuations by changing their retirement behavior.

Yet empirical analysis shows no consistent evidence that workers are more likely to retire early when they experience larger returns on their housing investments. Whereas workers aged sixty-two to sixty-nine appear responsive to stock market and labor market fluctuations, they do not respond to housing market fluctuations as expected in any of our models, nor do homeowners show a greater response than renters, as would also be expected.

One potential reason we were unable to identify an impact of house price fluctuations is that people may not routinely sell their homes after they retire and use the proceeds to finance their retirement consumption.[4] In fact, past studies support this. For instance, Venti and Wise (2004) find that most households do not sell their homes until they

---

4. More recently, reverse mortgages have emerged as an option that allows households to consume their housing wealth without selling their homes. Although these mortgages are becoming more popular over time, their use is still quite rare: in 2005, only 43,000 such mortgages were originated (Eschtruth, Sun, and Webb, 2006).

experience an event such as a spouse's death or entry into a nursing home. Some analysts therefore argue that many households treat their home equity as a "buffer stock" of wealth held to protect the household against the risk of shocks late in life. If this is how most older households operate, then it is not surprising that house price fluctuations do not appear to affect retirement behavior, despite assertions in the popular press to the contrary. As a result, it seems unnecessary to include any retirement response to the housing market crash in our simulations of the effect of current market conditions on retirement in chapter 8.

6 | *Impact of the Labor Market Crash*

According to the Social Security Administration's chief actuary, Stephen Goss, the number of claims for new retired worker benefits in late 2008 and early 2009 rose by 10 percent more than one would expect from changes in demographics alone (Goss, 2009). Goss suspected that the economic downturn was the potential cause of this unexpected increase. But if, as indicated in chapter 4, poor stock market returns are leading at least some workers to delay retirement, how can new Social Security claims (which are synonymous with retirement for many, though not all, workers) be on the rise?

One possible explanation is that the weakness in the labor market is eroding the jobs of older workers. Since the current crisis began, the economy has lost more than 7 million jobs. Older workers are certainly not immune from this phenomenon and may be less attractive to prospective employers if thought to have higher health care costs or to lack certain skills. The difficulty of finding new work may lead older workers to throw in the towel, file their Social Security claim to provide income support, and withdraw from the labor force.

These retiring workers are likely to be different from those delaying retirement in response to the stock market crash. The delayers are likely to be more affluent, since those with the most assets suffer the greatest loss when the stock market falls (see chapter 4). Those retiring early owing to a lost job will likely be less-skilled workers, who traditionally are at greater risk of job loss when the labor market falters. The aggregate impact of the economic crisis on retirement would be the net of the number of these workers retiring early and the number of higher-skilled workers delaying retirement because of their stock losses, if both these phenomena are in fact occurring.

To assess the impact of a weak labor market on the likelihood that an older worker will retire, one must first examine the labor market for older workers, particularly their unemployment experiences over the course of the business cycle and in relation to those of younger workers. The difficulty in relying on comparisons of the retirement patterns of those who differ by their unemployment experiences is that unemployment is not randomly assigned. Those who become unemployed may have had a greater propensity to retire early even in the absence of unemployment. Hence an empirical analysis is again needed to determine whether the loss of a job actually "causes" individuals to withdraw from the labor force and whether labor market conditions have a different effect on workers at different skill levels.

The Labor Market for Older Workers

The effect of the current economic crisis on the labor market has been hard to miss. Ever since the crisis began, the Bureau of Labor Statistics has issued a fresh installment of bad news in its monthly report, The Employment Situation: hundreds of thousands of additional lost jobs and further increases in the unemployment rate. With the loss of 7.3 million jobs between December of 2007 and November of 2009, the unemployment rate rose by 5.3 percentage points, and as 2009 came to a close, more than 10 percent of workers found themselves without jobs.

How unusual is the current situation by historical standards? Trends in the unemployment rate since 1970 (figure 6-1) show some very strong cyclical patterns, with seven recessions, as identified by spikes in the unemployment rate (technically, two occurred in the early 1980s). The

Figure 6-1. *U.S. Unemployment Rate over Time*

Unemployment rate

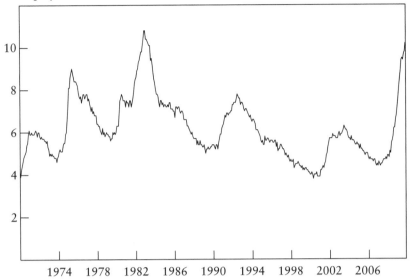

Source: Bureau of Labor Statistics.

period before the early 1980s witnessed largely a secular trend toward higher unemployment, interspersed with good years and bad years. The opposite occurred in the years that followed. Although some years were better than others, the unemployment rate was trending by and large downward over this period, falling to around 4 percent by the late 1990s. With the onset of the present economic crisis, the unemployment rate has neared its post–World War II peak of 10.8 percent, observed in the fall of 1982.

The labor market situation for older workers tends to follow similar patterns, but with considerably lower rates of unemployment (figure 6-2). When unemployment peaked in the early 1980s, the unemployment rate for workers between the ages of fifty-five and sixty-four hit an annual rate of 5.6 percent in 1982, compared with 7.9 percent for prime-age workers (twenty-five to fifty-four). The lower rates

Figure 6-2. *Annual Unemployment Rate for Workers, by Age*

Unemployment rate

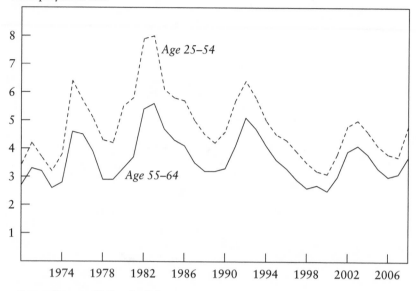

Source: Bureau of Labor Statistics.

for the older group could be related to two possible factors, each with very different implications for retirement behavior and workers' well-being. On the one hand, older workers are more likely to have settled into longer-term employment relationships that are less likely to come to an end when the economy sours. On the other hand, older workers who do lose their job during a recession may be pessimistic about their chances of finding new work and may choose to retire rather than look for new work. As such, they would not be counted as unemployed because they would not have met the work search requirements for such a designation. In this case, the lower unemployment rate experienced by older workers would tend to understate the hardship that they face as a group when the economy is weak.

Another potential problem in using the unemployment rate as a means of gauging how many older workers experience hardship during a recession is that it is a point-in-time measure. Each monthly survey captures individuals searching for work during the survey week. Over the course of a recession, as workers lose jobs and others find them, more workers experience unemployment at some point than are unemployed at a single point in time.

One way to explore this issue is to examine retrospective reports of the number of workers experiencing some period of unemployment in the past calendar year.[1] In March of each year, the Current Population Survey (CPS) asks about labor market activity in the past year in addition to its usual monthly questions about current labor market activity. An alternative measure of unemployment can be constructed by calculating the percentage of individuals in the labor force last year who were unemployed for at least some part of that year. This would do a better job of capturing the cumulative number of workers experiencing unemployment over some period. Although recessions frequently last longer than a year (at least this is true for the weakness in the labor market), the exposure to unemployment over one year nonetheless provides a better gauge of the total number of workers affected by the downturn than does a point-in-time measure of unemployment.

As one would expect, our calculations of these statistics (figure 6-3) exhibit the same cyclical patterns just discussed for the unemployment rate as traditionally measured. Older workers are again found to be less likely to experience unemployment than are prime-age workers. Yet the percentage of those experiencing some unemployment over the course of a year is considerably higher than the unemployment rate. The traditional unemployment rate for older workers peaked at 5.6 percent in the early 1980s, but this retrospective measure peaked at 10.3 percent. In good times, like the late 1990s, this statistic bottoms out at around 4 percent.

The extent to which older workers suffer in the labor market during recessions can similarly be observed by examining rates of job "displacement." Workers are said to be displaced if they become unemployed

1. Levine (1993) compares issues regarding an unemployment rate constructed in this manner with those arising from the traditional unemployment rate.

Figure 6-3. *Percentage of Workers Experiencing Unemployment in the Last Calendar Year, by Age*

Percent

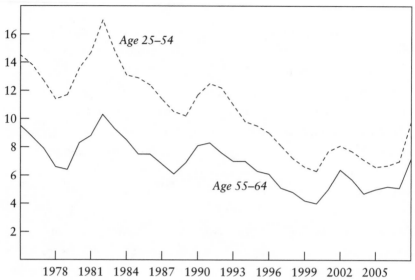

Source: Authors' calculations from March Current Population Surveys.

because their plant or company closed or moved, there was insufficient work for them to do, or their position or shift was abolished. Biennial supplements to the CPS ("the Displaced Worker Survey") beginning in 1984 have attempted to identify workers displaced in the three years preceding the survey. These data can be used to create a "displacement rate," which measures the percentage of workers displaced in that period.[2] Displacement rates clearly fluctuate over time (figure 6-4) in response to the business cycle. Furthermore, older workers experience a significant degree of job displacement. Over a three-year period, roughly 10 percent of those aged fifty to sixty-four are displaced when the labor

2. Changes in the specific design of the survey over time make it difficult to create uniform measures to estimate movements over time. Henry Farber (2010) undertook this task both recently (2007) and in a series of earlier papers. We report his data here to incorporate his solutions to the problem, which explains why the age ranges do not exactly match those in the remainder of the chapter.

Figure 6-4. *Job Displacement Rates, by Age*

Percentage of workers displaced in period

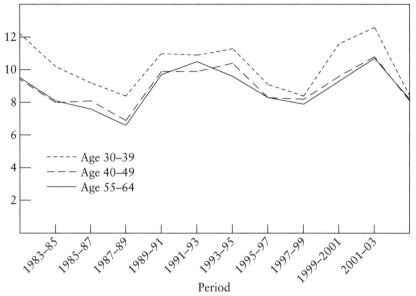

Source: Farber (2005).

market is weak. This rate is only somewhat lower than that for younger workers.

Regardless of the specific measure used, it is clear that recessions have a significant impact on employment outcomes for older workers. The next question to consider is whether business cycle conditions affect the likelihood of retirement.

Descriptive Analysis

As a first step, we examine whether older workers tend to retire when they become unemployed. This does not necessarily mean that the unemployment "caused" the retirement. The types of workers who are more likely to retire early also could be the ones who suffer more unemployment. The point here is to determine whether a correlation exists; later we focus on whether it is coincidental or causal.

During an economic downturn, as just discussed, older workers are somewhat less likely to be displaced than younger workers, but they are still displaced at substantial rates. What happens to these workers? Previous research has shown that displaced workers have great difficulty recovering from the event, suffering employment and earnings losses for quite some time (Jacobson, LaLonde, and Sullivan, 1993; von Wachter, Song, and Manchester, 2008). One "option" (perhaps not a very good one) is to withdraw from the labor force. For older workers, this could be thought of as retirement. An important question to answer, then, is whether older workers are more likely to withdraw from the labor force in the face of a job displacement than younger workers. At younger ages, workers who face many years without income support before they would become eligible for retirement benefits may continue to fight the uphill battle to find a job. At older ages, workers may just give up.

Statistics drawn from the Displaced Worker Survey suggest that this is the case.[3] Roughly 10 percent of prime-age workers (aged twenty-five to fifty-four) report withdrawing from the labor force following displacement, versus one-quarter of older workers aged fifty-five to sixty-four (figure 6-5). This suggests that retirement is reasonably common following displacement.

We also use data on retirement rates from the March CPS to further establish this relationship. These data make it possible to determine whether those who were in the labor force in the preceding calendar year have withdrawn from the labor force by March of the survey year. As described earlier, we consider these transitions to be retirements and call the transition rate a retirement "hazard."

When these retirement hazard rates are calculated by exact age over the period 1980 through 2007 (figure 6-6), we find that they increase at older ages, with pronounced spikes at ages sixty-two and sixty-five, ages that are associated with Social Security provisions. For the present

---

3. Earlier surveys asked about job displacement in the past five years, and more recent surveys examine the past three years. This distinction is likely to explain the higher rates of labor force withdrawal in the early years, as displayed in figure 6-5.

Figure 6-5. *Percentage of Displaced Workers Who Withdrew from the Labor Force, by Survey Date, by Age*

Percent

Source: Authors' calculations from the 1984–2008 Displaced Worker Survey.

purposes, however, the important point is the difference between those who experienced some unemployment in the preceding calendar year and those who did not. Retirement rates are much higher for the former group. At age sixty-two, for instance, one-quarter of workers who experienced some unemployment in the preceding calendar year retired by the March survey date. Only 15 percent of workers who were not unemployed in the preceding year retired at this age.

We can use the same data to compare retirement rates over time by unemployment status, pooling together workers aged fifty-five to sixty-nine (figure 6-7). Overall, the conclusion is similar to that from the previous figure: those who were exposed to a spell of unemployment during the past year are considerably more likely to retire than those who were not. Interestingly, workers who experience no unemployment show a noticeable trend toward lower retirement rates over time.

Figure 6-6. *Empirical Retirement Hazard Rates, by Age and Unemployment Status, 1980–2007*

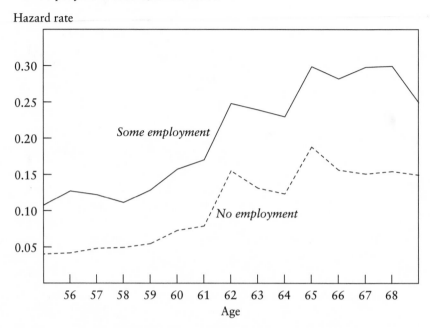

Source: Authors' calculations from March Current Population Surveys.

Annual retirement rates for these workers are about 10 percent in the beginning of the sample period but start to decline in the early 1990s, reaching a level of 6 percent by 2007. This pattern is consistent with the recent trend toward greater labor force participation among older workers highlighted in chapter 2. No such pattern exists among workers who experience some unemployment. For them, retirement rates remain roughly constant (albeit a bit noisy because of smaller sample sizes) at about 15 percent. This suggests that whatever factors are driving many workers to remain in the labor force longer, they are not influencing the behavior of unemployed older workers.[4] This would

4. Friedberg and Webb (2005) argue that the shift from defined benefit to defined contribution pensions can explain some of this increase; Gustman and Steinmeier (2008) make a similar argument with respect to changes in Social Security rules.

Figure 6-7. *Empirical Retirement Hazard Rates over Time,*
by Employment Status, Workers Aged Fifty-Five to Sixty-Nine

Hazard rate

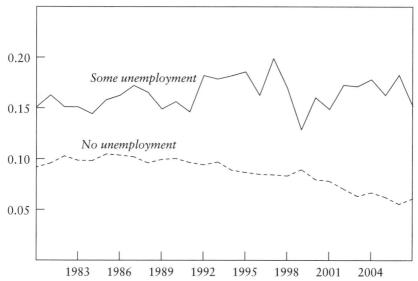

Source: Authors' calculations from March Current Population Surveys.

lead one to believe that other constraints may be dominating their behavior. Thus it appears that unemployment plays an important role in the retirement process for some workers, although further investigation is required to establish a causal link.

Empirical Analysis

Drawing on thirty years of CPS data, we relate the likelihood that an individual will retire to the labor market conditions that existed in his or her state of residence at the time. We hold constant state-specific factors that tend to lead workers to retire earlier in some states than in others at any point in the business cycle (such as industrial composition or climate), year-specific factors that increase retirement rates nationwide in some years relative to others, and differences in individual characteristics (demographics, including age and education) that increase the propensity of some workers to retire sooner than others. This approach provides an indication of whether workers retire earlier when the labor market is weaker in their "locality" (that is, state) after all of these other differences are taken into account.

Note that it is uncertain what impact a weaker labor market will have on retirement behavior. As we have stated throughout this volume, we hypothesize that a weak labor market may lead some individuals to retire (albeit involuntarily) because of their inability to find work after becoming unemployed. Alternatively, workers with jobs who may have otherwise considered retiring may be reluctant to do so. This could happen if uncertainty surrounds their decision and they want to be able return to work should they find they are not happy being retired (because of insufficient income or the need to find something to keep themselves occupied, for instance). If they are not confident in their ability to find new work, they may be less likely to retire. In addition, some older individuals may find themselves leaving retirement and looking for work again if, for instance, their spouse loses a job. We estimate the net of all of these effects.

Another relevant point concerns the magnitude of these effects. From the discussion so far, we have been able to determine that although a greater number of older workers experience the hardship of unemployment during a recession than during other periods, the actual number of additional workers affected by even a bad recession is probably only about 5 percent. The vast majority of older workers will not experience unemployment. Among the additional 5 percent who are affected, only some of these workers will choose to retire as a result of becoming unemployed. As a result, it would be implausible to estimate a very large impact of labor market conditions on retirement behavior. Individuals retire for a lot of reasons, and the additional unemployed workers that are led to retire as a result over the course of a recession could only feasibly change average retirement rates by a relatively small amount. This could explain why we see no cyclical fluctuations in retirement rates in aggregate retirement trends, such as those displayed in figure 3-1. The question is whether our statistical methods are sufficient to enable us to

Figure 6-8. *Baseline Retirement Hazard Rates, by Age and Educational Attainment*

Retirement hazard rate

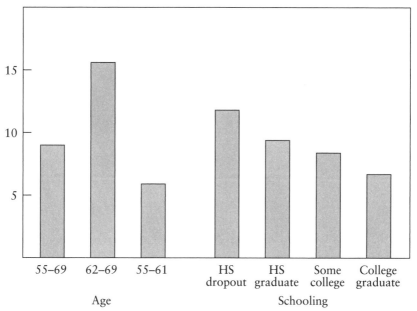

Source: Authors' calculations from March Current Population Surveys.

capture the effect of a recession on retirements even though we do not expect those effects to be very large for the population as a whole.

To place our subsequent analysis into context, we first calculate baseline average retirement rates for workers of all ages (fifty-five to sixty-nine) over the full sample period (1980 through 2007), and then separately by age group and level of educational attainment. As shown in figure 6-8, the average retirement rate for this age group is 9 percent a year. In other words, for every 100 individuals in the group working at the beginning of the year, 9 will retire over the course of the year. Not surprisingly, this rate is higher for workers aged sixty-two to sixty-nine than for workers aged fifty-five to sixty-one. In fact, the older group retires at almost three times the rate of the younger group. Retirement rates differ across workers with different levels of educational attainment as well. Those who never graduated from high school retire at almost twice the rate of those who have graduated from college.

In estimating the impact of a major recession on retirement rates, we assume an increase in the unemployment rate of 5 percentage points, which is roughly what the nation has experienced to date in the current recession. We conduct this exercise for our full sample as well as by age and educational attainment subcategories.

We estimate that a major recession will increase the retirement rate for the full sample by 0.9 percentage points (see figure 6-9).[5] From the sample's baseline retirement of 9 percent (see figure 6-8), it appears that retirements would increase by 10 percent in response to a major recession. When the sample is divided by age, one finds this result is driven largely by the older group. The retirement rate for those sixty-two to sixty-nine years old is estimated to rise by 1.8 percentage points. From a baseline retirement hazard rate of 15.6 percent, this represents a 12 percent increase. The estimated impact for those fifty-five to sixty-one is smaller and is not statistically significant.

In past work (Coile and Levine, 2007), we have disaggregated the age groups further and found that a systematic and statistically significant response of retirement rates to labor market conditions begins precisely at age sixty-two. The fact that this is the age at which individuals first become eligible for Social Security retirement benefits (albeit at a reduced rate compared with what workers receive when they wait until their normal retirement age to claim) strongly suggests that the availability of those benefits plays a role in that decision.

As for the role of educational attainment, workers with only a high school degree appear to experience the largest estimated effect of a major recession. This is also the only group for which we estimate an impact that is statistically significantly different from zero. The magnitude of this effect is fairly large; a 5 percentage point increase in the unemployment rate is estimated to increase the retirement rate of this

5. The exact statistics on which this figure is based are available in Coile and Levine (2009).

Figure 6-9. *Impact of Major Recession on Retirement Rates,*
by Age and Educational Attainment[a]

Impact on retirement hazard rate

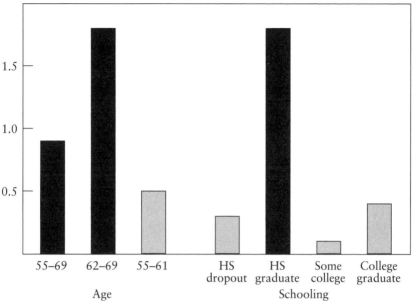

Source: Authors' calculations from March Current Population Surveys.
a. Statistically significant results are shaded in black and insignificant results in gray.

group of workers by 1.8 percentage points. With a baseline retirement
rate of 9.4 percent, this reflects a 19 percent increase in retirements.

These results seem plausible on the basis of the different labor market realities that exist for workers who have received different levels of
education. The key factors that matter are the ability to continue working to older ages, the likelihood of unemployment when a recession
occurs, and the ability to obtain new employment should unemployment occur. High school dropouts are the likeliest to lose their jobs in
a recession and may have the hardest time finding new jobs. But these
individuals may also be in poorer health and may be employed in more
physically demanding jobs, so they may be more likely to retire at early
ages anyway. High school graduates may have the right combination of
a desire to continue working along with a higher risk of unemployment

and difficulty in finding new work, so a recession may lead many of them to retire involuntarily. For more skilled workers, the risk of unemployment during a recession may not be high enough to lead many of them to retire during an economic downturn.

Summary and Conclusions

Labor market factors clearly play an important role in determining workers' retirement decisions. Our descriptive analysis shows that older workers who become unemployed are more likely to retire. However, it is difficult to determine from this evidence alone whether they are retiring earlier than they otherwise would as a result of becoming unemployed. Without an available counterfactual, the relationship cannot be considered causal with any degree of certainty. Through more sophisticated empirical analysis designed to determine whether higher unemployment rates in a worker's state of residence "cause" them to retire earlier than they would have otherwise, we found strong support for the hypothesis that individuals—particularly those over the age of sixty-two and with only a high school degree—do retire earlier when recessions hit.

How large, then, would the effect of a weak labor market be in the current economic downturn, and how does the magnitude of this effect compare with that of other market influences on retirement? As discussed in the foregoing chapters, longer-term declines in the value of stocks lead workers, particularly those at the top of the economic spectrum, to delay retirement, whereas housing markets do not appear to alter retirement decisions. We examine the decrease in retirement that one would expect as a result of falling stock prices and the increase that we would expect from the weak labor market in detail in chapter 8.

7 | *Implications for Retiree Well-Being*

An important conclusion from chapters 4, 5, and 6 is that weaker longer-term stock returns lead more-skilled workers to delay retirement, while higher unemployment rates lead the less-skilled to seek earlier retirement. By contrast, housing market returns do not appear to have much impact on retirement behavior.

So far our analysis has focused exclusively on the effect of market fluctuations on retirement. Retirement is certainly an important subject, as indicated by the voluminous research on its determinants. It also is of great interest to policymakers. Public policy can play an important role in influencing retirement decisions, and conversely, individual retirement decisions can have implications for public policy. For instance, a trend toward earlier retirement alters projections of Social Security trust fund balances, at least in the short term. Retirement behavior also has important macroeconomic implications: fewer workers mean lower gross domestic product (GDP).

Ultimately, however, our primary concern in studying the retirement response to various market conditions is its impact on the subsequent well-being of individuals. If individuals retire earlier or later than they anticipated but are just as well off in retirement (and we mean that in the broadest possible sense at this point), then it may not matter very much when they retire.

But how does one assess well-being? Although a number of possible measures of well-being might merit attention, we were guided by practical considerations regarding what measures actually exist in surveys with large enough sample sizes that are available over long enough periods of time to allow us to assess the impact of changing market conditions. Given that this is a significant constraint on our options, as described later in this chapter, our most viable alternative is to examine the impact of market conditions around the time of retirement on an individual's income in retirement.

By way of a consistency check on our formal statistical analysis, we conduct thought exercises designed to illustrate the extent to which changing market conditions could alter income in retirement. These exercises help us to determine whether our findings are plausible. We focus on changes in stock market and labor market conditions. The impact of changes in housing markets on retiree well-being should be negligible, since few households use housing equity to finance their retirement spending (see chapter 6).

How Does One Measure Well-Being?

Economists use the notion of "utility" as a conceptual measure of an individual's well-being. When an individual who has the option of retiring at any date chooses a particular date, it is assumed to be the one that provides the greatest utility for that individual. Working longer than expected or withdrawing from the labor market earlier than expected in response to an unexpected negative shock, such as a spell of unemployment or a drop in the value of the worker's portfolio, will make the individual worse off. In theory, therefore, well-being would certainly be expected to decrease whenever retirement decisions change in response to deteriorating market conditions.

The trouble arises when one tries to measure this. Unfortunately, the useful theoretical construct of utility does not translate into something that is easily measured in the real world. This raises the thorny question of how one can tell whether, and to what extent, individuals are worse off if they alter their retirement decisions in response to changing market conditions. Utility needs to be replaced with something that is easier to grasp.

Some studies measure an individual's "happiness." In essence, this construct of well-being closely resembles the idea of utility, but the data are too limited for our purposes because the existing surveys that include this measure do not cover the number of respondents that we would need.

Another possibility might be to measure the things that economists usually think of as determining one's utility. This list might include leisure, health, and consumption.

Leisure is something that can be observed and that clearly has value, so retiring earlier than expected can bring some benefits of this nature to individuals. These additional benefits would need to be weighed against other factors (such as any changes in health or consumption) in order to determine the net effect of an early retirement on well-being. Despite its relevance, however, focusing on leisure raises the problem of how to measure its value. For younger workers, it would be commonplace to use the individual's wage rate to determine the value of leisure, since that worker is trading off labor for leisure, making the wage rate implicitly equal to the value of leisure. For older workers with fewer labor market opportunities, however, it is less clear that this is the right approach.

Health status is another factor that is easy to observe (although it might not be available in surveys with large enough samples to suit our needs) and clearly contributes to an individual's well-being. Retiring earlier or later than expected may alter one's health status and hence one's well-being. On the other hand, valuing health status is hard to do. If health solely entailed life expectancy, then some value of living an extra year could be constructed to measure the impact on well-being. But that is a controversial approach. Valuing changes in one's quality of life presents an even greater challenge.

Consumption is a term economists use to represent all the things one buys in the marketplace and consumes. It is an aggregate commodity—

the entire contents of one's shopping cart. To the extent that individuals derive happiness from having these items, consumption is an important component of utility. Retiring earlier or later than one expects certainly could influence one's subsequent consumption in retirement because this decision would affect one's finances. Having more or less money available to buy goods will affect consumption and therefore utility. Consumption, however, is also difficult to measure on a large scale. Surveys of individual consumption behavior do exist, but they are not of the scale required for the analysis we have in mind.

A measure that is readily available to us, however, is an individual's income in retirement. Clearly, one's retirement decision can have an impact there. Economists, however, tend not to view income as something that provides utility on its own, but rather as something valuable because of its ability to fund consumption. Income and consumption are certainly related, but not necessarily perfectly. Consumption from savings (or borrowing) is possible and will generate a gap between income and consumption. If the individual receives "in-kind" goods—for example, free health insurance—this creates a further disconnect between income and consumption. If we were able to observe consumption directly, we would prefer to use that, but unfortunately such information is not available on the scale necessary for our purposes. By contrast, income data are available on a very large scale, as described in chapter 3. In view of the options open to us, the most viable alternative is to examine the impact of changing market conditions on an individual's income in retirement.

Although this measure has some drawbacks as well, income is an important component of well-being in its own right and is likely to be the first thing that comes to mind when one thinks about economic well-being. Income and consumption are certainly very highly correlated, even if not perfectly so: increases in income almost always lead to increases in consumption. Without ignoring the problems of focusing exclusively on income, we believe that it is a tremendously important outcome to consider.

How Much Can Changing Market Conditions Matter?

If a worker is forced to retire prematurely as the result of a layoff, what can be expected to happen to his or her retirement income? What impact would a 50 percent decline in the stock market have? How do these effects vary across individuals at different locations in the income distribution? Some "back-of-the-envelope" calculations can assist with the interpretation of our subsequent empirical findings.

Our analysis is based on the descriptive statistics in chapter 3 (see table 3-1) showing mean personal income levels for retired men in their seventies by income type (Social Security, investment, pension, and other) and by income category (top, middle, and bottom third of the income distribution). In the present exercise, we ignore pension income because this source of income represents mainly payments from defined benefit plans, which are unlikely to be dramatically affected by changing market conditions.[1] As described in chapter 3, an average male retiree in his seventies receives $34,000 in total income, with $11,000 coming from Social Security and $8,000 coming from investments.

We now make a straightforward calculation of the lost income that would result from changing market conditions based on the assumption that individuals experience a 20 percent loss of Social Security income and a 25 percent loss of investment income. The loss in Social Security income is the reduction in benefits a worker would experience by claiming benefits at age sixty-two instead of sixty-five (sixty-five being the Social Security "normal retirement age" for all workers

---

1. Pension income could include distributions from defined contribution pensions as well, which could be affected by changing market conditions. We ignore this possibility for two reasons. First, payments from these pensions may be reported as investment income because the entity making the payment is likely to be an investment firm. Second, defined benefit pensions are a more important source of pension wealth even among those in their fifties (Gustman, Steinmeier, and Tabatabai, 2009), suggesting that older workers are even more likely to be reliant on defined benefit pensions.

Table 7-1. *Simulated Impact of Changing Market Conditions on Retirement Income, by Location in Total Personal Income Distribution, Dollars*

		Social Security income			Investment income		
Group	Total personal income (1)	Observed (2)	Impact of 20 percent reduction (3)	Percentage impact on total income (4)	Observed (5)	Impact of 25 percent reduction (6)	Percentage impact on total income (7)
All	34,034	11,388	–2,278	–6.7	8,066	–2,017	–5.9
Bottom third	9,686	7,807	–1,561	–16.1	306	–77	–0.8
Middle third	23,032	12,673	–2,535	–11.0	2,261	–565	–2.5
Top third	68,356	13,621	–2,724	–4.0	21,234	–5,309	–7.8

Source: Authors' calculations from the 2000 Census and 2001–07 American Community Surveys.

in our data).[2] Essentially, we are assuming that an unexpected layoff would lead a worker to retire and claim three years earlier than planned. For investment income, the 25 percent reduction in this income source is the loss that would result if a retired worker had 50 percent of his or her portfolio invested in stocks and the stock market declined by 50 percent.

As reported in table 7-1, an average retiree hit by a 20 percent reduction in Social Security benefits will lose $2,278, which represents 6.7 percent of total annual income. An average retiree experiencing a 25 percent decline in investment income suffers a loss of $2,017 a year, which represents 5.9 percent of total income.

The magnitudes of these effects are similar, but the distributional implications are very different. For retirees in the bottom third of the income distribution, a 20 percent reduction in Social Security benefits amounts to 16 percent of their total annual income, which is less than $10,000 to start with. This income loss would impose a substantial burden on these individuals. But they would be unaffected by changes in stock market conditions, which is not surprising since workers at this income level are unlikely to hold stocks.

2. Currently, the normal retirement age is sixty-six, and those who retire at age sixty-two face a 25 percent reduction in their monthly benefit.

Individuals in the top third of the income distribution would suffer a somewhat larger loss in dollar terms than low-income individuals if their Social Security benefits were reduced by 20 percent; however, this represents a considerably smaller proportion of their total income than was the case for low-income individuals. For high-income individuals, the bigger impact would come from a decline in investment income. A 25 percent reduction in this source of income would cost these retirees more than $5,000 a year. This represents a 7.8 percent drop in their total income.

The lesson from this simulation is that the largest potential risk from the economic crisis is that lower-income workers will suffer a substantial reduction in their Social Security benefits as the result of retiring earlier than expected. We now consider whether the intuition from this simulation bears out in the real world.

The Impact of Market Conditions on Retiree Income

Although our methods here are similar to those described in chapter 3, they are not identical because our central concern now is retiree well-being in the years following the retirement decision. We therefore focus on the retirement income of individuals who are between the ages of seventy and seventy-nine. The vast majority of workers retire earlier than this, so focusing on this age group makes it possible to examine income levels, abstracting from the retirement decision itself. Our goal is to assess the effect of economic conditions that existed around the time of retirement on subsequent retiree well-being for this group.

Methodology

The first issue to resolve is what we mean by "around the time of retirement." We do not mean the actual time of retirement, of course, for we simply do not know that in our data.[3] When we refer to labor market

3. Even if we did know the exact age of retirement, we would not want to use it anyway. Those who are willing to live on less and who enjoy work less may retire earlier. If those preferences have any time series and regional variation, or both, they may be correlated with changes in market conditions. We would rather

conditions, we use the unemployment rate that existed when each retiree was sixty-two years old. This is a reasonable age to choose because retirement rates spike at that age anyway when individuals first become eligible for Social Security (see chapter 3). Moreover, our past work (Coile and Levine, 2007, 2009) has shown that the impact of labor market conditions on retirement decisions does not begin until age sixty-two, further supporting this decision.

When it comes to stock market conditions around the time of retirement, the relevant time frame becomes less clear conceptually. Market conditions may matter, but they could matter at any point leading up to (or even after) the retirement decision, not just right at that point. If a worker's retirement nest egg doubles or even triples in his or her fifties, that certainly paves the way toward an earlier retirement and higher retirement income, even if the worker does not actually retire until age sixty-two. We take a more agnostic approach in deciding what period to use for stock market conditions: we use the five-year real rate of return in the S&P 500 starting in the year the respondent turned age fifty, fifty-five, sixty, and sixty-five (representing returns between fifty and fifty-five, fifty-five and sixty, sixty and sixty-five, and sixty-five and seventy). As shown in our past work, retirement decisions are more likely to respond to longer-term changes in market returns, including those at a five-year interval, which justifies our use of returns calculated over this span. With a sample of individuals aged seventy and up, it seems reasonable to work backward from there in selecting the returns to use.

Another important point about our data is that we restrict our attention to the income levels of male retirees. We do not intend to understate the importance of the well-being of older women. In fact, we recognize that some aspects of retiree well-being are more important to understand for women than for men. For instance, the poverty rate of older widows is almost twice as high as that for the broader elderly population

---

assign market conditions to workers around the time of retirement using alternative, exogenous measures that still may capture the market constraints workers face when they consider retirement.

(McGarry and Schoeni, 2005). Additional analyses of this group would be of great value.

The difficulty this segment of the population poses for our analysis is the lack of data, particularly as they pertain to rules that govern Social Security benefits. For an individual worker, these benefits are calculated on the basis of one's own work history. Benefits are also available for dependent or surviving spouses of workers. Among the current elderly population, where men were the primary earners in the family, Social Security benefits will be tied by and large to the husband's work history and his retirement age. This means that market conditions when the husband was approaching retirement may be more relevant. However, we do not have any information about the husband if he has passed away. In our data, 43 percent of women between the ages of seventy-one and eighty are widows. To circumvent this problem, we focus on the income levels of men, the vast majority of whom are collecting Social Security benefits based on their own work history.

To return to the issue of the counterfactual, we use methods similar to those described earlier in the book. Just as there were substantial differences in the probability of retirement at different ages, there may be an age pattern in retirement income; for example, income may fall with age if workers consume some of their assets in early retirement and have declining investment income thereafter. Retirement income also may have a pattern over time as, for instance, current stock market conditions fluctuate and alter income flows from investments. Geographic differences in retirement income may also exist that are related to overall income differences across states. Our statistical approach controls for all such differences across retirees.

For this application, we take advantage of the fact that in any given survey year our sample from the Census and ACS data (described in chapter 3) will contain retirees who will have reached retirement age at different points in time. This is due to the fact that our data cover retirees aged seventy-one to eighty (reporting income in the years they were seventy to seventy-nine) in every year rather than retirees of a single age at a point in time.

Table 7-2. *Year Survey Respondents were Born, by Year of Survey and Age in Survey Year*

Age in survey year	Survey year							
	2000	2001	2002	2003	2004	2005	2006	2007
71	1929	1930	1931	1932	1933	1934	1935	1936
72	1928	1929	1930	1931	1932	1933	1934	1935
73	1927	1928	1929	1930	1931	1932	1933	1934
74	1926	1927	1928	1929	1930	1931	1932	1933
75	1925	1926	1927	1928	1929	1930	1931	1932
76	1924	1925	1926	1927	1928	1929	1930	1931
77	1923	1924	1925	1926	1927	1928	1929	1930
78	1922	1923	1924	1925	1926	1927	1928	1929
79	1921	1922	1923	1924	1925	1926	1927	1928
80	1920	1921	1922	1923	1924	1925	1926	1927

To illustrate this point, we tabulate the year of birth for individuals of each of these ages for each survey year between 2000 and 2007 and record the year in which each individual reached age sixty-two (table 7-2). For instance, a retiree who was seventy-four years old when surveyed in 2004 was born in 1930, so he or she would have been sixty-two in the year 1992 (table 7-3). A seventy-eight-year-old retiree in that same survey would have been born in 1926 and reached age sixty-two in 1988. Because both were surveyed in the same year, any difference in their income cannot be attributed to the survey year. However, differences in the unemployment rate they faced around the time of retirement (at age sixty-two) may help to explain any difference in their retirement incomes. The unemployment rates at age sixty-two for these two workers were 7.5 percent and 5.5 percent, respectively (table 7-4). Differences such as these enable us to determine the impact of unemployment at age sixty-two on current retiree income, holding constant contemporaneous factors (such as today's stock market prices) that may affect both retirees.

To hold age constant, similar comparisons can be made across survey years for workers of the same age, drawing on tables 7-2 to 7-4. For example, we can compare one seventy-five-year-old retiree surveyed in 2002 and another surveyed in 2006 to examine the relation-

Table 7-3. *Year Survey Respondents Turned Age Sixty-Two,*
by Year of Survey and Age in Survey Year

Age in survey year	Survey year							
	2000	*2001*	*2002*	*2003*	*2004*	*2005*	*2006*	*2007*
71	1991	1992	1993	1994	1995	1996	1997	1998
72	1990	1991	1992	1993	1994	1995	1996	1997
73	1989	1990	1991	1992	1993	1994	1995	1996
74	1988	1989	1990	1991	1992	1993	1994	1995
75	1987	1988	1989	1990	1991	1992	1993	1994
76	1986	1987	1988	1989	1990	1991	1992	1993
77	1985	1986	1987	1988	1989	1990	1991	1992
78	1984	1985	1986	1987	1988	1989	1990	1991
79	1983	1984	1985	1986	1987	1988	1989	1990
80	1982	1983	1984	1985	1986	1987	1988	1989

ship between the unemployment rates that existed when they were age sixty-two (5.3 percent for the worker who was seventy-five in 2002 and hence sixty-two in 1989, versus 6.9 percent for the worker who was seventy-five in 2006 and hence sixty-two in 1993) and their retirement income on the survey date, to see whether these two factors are related. Since both workers are the same age, this approach enables us to abstract from general aging patterns that may affect retirement income.

Comparable exercises can be used to estimate the impact of changes in stock market conditions on retiree income. We use the variation in the real rates of return between ages fifty-five and sixty for the relevant birth cohorts in each survey year (table 7-5) to estimate the impact of stock market returns at different ages on retirement income. We also include real rates of return between ages fifty and fifty-five, sixty and sixty-five, and sixty-five and seventy in a similar manner.

Although our specific methods are more sophisticated than those described here, this discussion illustrates how the data at our disposal can be used to simulate the notion of an experimental analysis. A full discussion of our methodology and results is available in Coile and Levine (2010).

Table 7-4. *National Unemployment Rate at Age Sixty-Two,*
by Year of Survey and Age in Survey Year

Age in survey year	Survey year							
	2000	2001	2002	2003	2004	2005	2006	2007
71	6.8	7.5	6.9	6.1	5.6	5.4	4.9	4.5
72	5.6	6.8	7.5	6.9	6.1	5.6	5.4	4.9
73	5.3	5.6	6.8	7.5	6.9	6.1	5.6	5.4
74	5.5	5.3	5.6	6.8	7.5	6.9	6.1	5.6
75	6.2	5.5	5.3	5.6	6.8	7.5	6.9	6.1
76	7	6.2	5.5	5.3	5.6	6.8	7.5	6.9
77	7.2	7	6.2	5.5	5.3	5.6	6.8	7.5
78	7.5	7.2	7	6.2	5.5	5.3	5.6	6.8
79	9.6	7.5	7.2	7	6.2	5.5	5.3	5.6
80	9.7	9.6	7.5	7.2	7	6.2	5.5	5.3

Results

Our reported results focus exclusively on Social Security and investment income.[4] One of the principal findings here is that changing labor
market conditions have little impact on the probability of the receipt of
Social Security but do affect the amount received by beneficiaries. The
lack of an effect on receipt is perhaps not surprising, since most (91 percent) of workers in this age group collect benefits and would presumably
do so regardless of market conditions. On the other hand, workers, on
average, experience a $21 loss in this source of income if the unem-
ployment rate rises by one point (table 7-6).

This number is somewhat difficult to interpret because only 1 extra
worker in 100 becomes unemployed if the unemployment rate rises by
one point. However, what we care about is the effect of unemployment
on income for that 1 affected worker, not the average effect for 100 work-

4. As foreshadowed from table 7-1, market conditions do not appear to have
any bearing on measured pension income. This may be due to the fact that defined
benefit pensions do not respond to market conditions, that defined benefit pensions are more prevalent among this age group, or that it is not clear whether
defined contribution pensions are reported as pension or investment income.

Table 7-5. *Real Percentage Increase in S&P 500 between Ages Fifty-Five and Sixty, by Year of Survey and Age in Survey Year*

Age in survey year	Survey year							
	2000	2001	2002	2003	2004	2005	2006	2007
71	76.6	27.5	38.1	43.2	38.6	9.3	62.7	54.3
72	41.5	76.6	27.5	38.1	43.2	38.6	9.3	62.7
73	48.5	41.5	76.6	27.5	38.1	43.2	38.6	9.3
74	67.8	48.5	41.5	76.6	27.5	38.1	43.2	38.6
75	22.8	67.8	48.5	41.5	76.6	27.5	38.1	43.2
76	12.9	22.8	67.8	48.5	41.5	76.6	27.5	38.1
77	14.9	12.9	22.8	67.8	48.5	41.5	76.6	27.5
78	−5.7	14.9	12.9	22.8	67.8	48.5	41.5	76.6
79	−29.2	−5.7	14.9	12.9	22.8	67.8	48.5	41.5
80	−3.1	−29.2	−5.7	14.9	12.9	22.8	67.8	48.5

ers, 99 of whom did not become unemployed when the unemployment rate went up. Therefore we convert this number (table 7-6, column 4) to the estimated income loss for an unemployed worker by multiplying the average aggregate loss (table 7-6, column 3) by 100. Now we see that the average worker who becomes unemployed in the period leading up to retirement loses $2,084 in annual Social Security income. Presumably this is attributable to earlier claiming of Social Security benefits.

Estimated income losses from Social Security are even higher for those in the bottom third of the income distribution, amounting to just over $3,000 for this group. Those at the top of the income distribution experience essentially no loss of benefits. These losses translate to an 18 percent drop in Social Security income for all workers and a 32 percent drop for retirees in the bottom third of the income distribution (column 5). In terms of the effect on total income, these losses represent a 6 percent drop for all workers and a 31 percent drop for lower-income retirees (column 6).

These results are similar in some ways to those in table 7-1. We predicted a comparable income loss overall, but somewhat smaller losses for the bottom third of the distribution and bigger losses for the top

Table 7-6. *Estimated Impact of Changing Market Conditions on Social Security Income for Those Receiving Benefits, by Location in Total Personal Income Distribution*

Group	Mean observed total personal income (1)	Mean observed Social Security income (conditional on receipt) (2)	Aggregate impact of a 1 point increase in the unemployment rate (3)	Impact of unemployment for an individual (4)	Percentage impact on Social Security income (5)	Percentage impact on total income (6)
All	34,034	11,388	–21	–2,084	–18.3	–6.1
Bottom third	9,686	9,343	–30	–3,006	–32.2	–31.0
Middle third	23,032	13,299	–20	–2,043	–15.4	–8.9
Top third	68,356	14,533	0	12	0.1	0.0

Source: Authors' calculations from the 2000 Census and 2001–07 American Community Surveys.

third of the income distribution than reported in table 7-6. In reality, unemployment may have minimal effect on retirement income for the most affluent group of retirees because they are subject to very low unemployment risk over the course of the business cycle. If these workers suffer relatively little additional unemployment when the aggregate unemployment rate rises, then their Social Security–claiming behavior will change very little, so their subsequent Social Security income in retirement will be largely unaffected.

For the least affluent retirees, estimates in table 7-6 may exceed predictions in table 7-1, for several reasons. First, the difference could be a statistical artifact; it may be that the true value of this estimate really is the same as in table 7-1, but random variation in the data led to this somewhat higher finding. Second, our simulation in table 7-1 was built on the premise that the additional unemployed worker claimed Social Security at age sixty-two rather than age sixty-five. However, perhaps he would have retired even later than sixty-five (say, at age sixty-six or sixty-seven) if he had not lost his job. Either way, our interpretation of these findings is that they are large, but not implausibly so.

In a comparable analysis of investment income (table 7-7), changes in stock market conditions have the greatest impact when they occur between ages fifty-five and sixty. Furthermore, these changes primarily affect the probability of receiving this form of income in retirement, not the amount received per recipient. As a result, we focus on changes in the average amount of income that individuals collectively receive when stock market returns change, which incorporates changes in the probability of receipt.

From table 7-7, it appears that a 50 percent decline in stock prices between the ages of fifty-five and sixty will reduce average incomes of retirees by $1,756.[5] This reflects a 21.8 percent reduction in income

5. Our empirical analysis actually examines the impact of an additional 1 percentage point change in the real rate of return on stocks over the five-year interval. On the basis of observed five-year real rates of return (shown in table 7-5), the swing from a very bad market exposure to a very good market exposure is around 100 points. A 100-point positive swing in stock prices reflects a doubling

Table 7-7. *Estimated Impact of Changing Market Conditions on Investment Income, by Location in Total Personal Income Distribution*

Group	Mean observed total personal income ($) (1)	Mean observed investment income ($) (2)	Impact of 50 percent decline in stock prices, ages 55–60 ($) (3)	Percentage impact on investment income (4)	Percentage impact on total income (5)
All	34,034	8,066	–1,756	–21.8	–5.2
Bottom third	9,686	306	–269	–87.9	–2.8
Middle third	23,032	2,261	–105	–4.6	–0.5
Top third	68,356	21,234	–2,266	–10.7	–3.3

Source: Authors' calculations from the 2000 Census and 2001–07 American Community Surveys.

from investments (column 4) and a 5.2 percent reduction in total income (column 5), on average.

As in our earlier calculations of the estimated impact of unemployment, the effect of falling stock prices is similar in magnitude to the 25 percent reduction in investment income simulated in table 7-1. This value was chosen to incorporate a 50 percent reduction in stock values along with an investment portfolio that had half of its assets in stocks. The average investment income in that simulation would fall by $2,017 (table 7-1), reflecting a 5.9 percent reduction in total income. This is very similar to the actual experiences of the seventy- to seventy-nine-year-old retirees in table 7-7.

When we examine the impact of a large stock market decline on investment income separately by income group, investment income drops significantly for those at the bottom of the distribution. But individuals at this level have so little investment income in the first place that this represents only a small change in their total income. Similarly, middle-income individuals experience a trivial reduction in their total retirement income in response to a stock market crash in the years leading up to their retirement. Most strongly affected are those at the top of the distribution, which is not surprising since this is the only group to receive much investment income in retirement. For them, a 50 percent decline in the value of the stock market between the ages of fifty-five and sixty results in a $2,266 loss in annual retirement income (table 7-7). Even with this sizable loss, however, total income drops only 3.3 percent, a small effect. Those retirees who have large investment incomes have large flows of income from other sources as well, so they can absorb the loss in income generated from a stock market crash without great difficulty.

---

of stock values. If that same dollar amount were lost rather than gained, it would reflect a 50 percent reduction. Therefore, the numbers in table 7-5, column 3, are actually the negative values of a 100 percentage point increase in five-year market returns.

Conclusions

Market conditions around the time of retirement appear to have long-lasting effects on the well-being of retirees. Without much ability to alter income streams once they retire, individuals who are exposed to high unemployment or falling stock prices as they approach retirement run the risk of reduced income for the remainder of their lives.

Although weakness in both the labor market and the stock market reduce economic well-being in retirement, their distributional impacts are very different. Those lower down in the income distribution are more likely to be affected by the higher levels of job loss in an economic downturn. Conversely, stock market fluctuations harm the retirement well-being of those higher in the income distribution because these individuals hold substantial amounts of stocks.

As a percentage of income, however, the cost associated with unemployment is substantially higher than that associated with falling stock prices. A lower-income worker who loses his or her job as retirement is approaching is subject to a reduction in subsequent retirement income of upward of 30 percent. Those at higher income levels who experience sharp market declines face retirement income losses on the order of a few percent. These findings are consistent with those regarding retirement behavior itself reported in chapters 4 through 6 and strongly suggest that the hardships experienced by older individuals with lower socioeconomic status need to receive more attention in the current economic crisis.

8 | *Discussion and Policy Implications*

The research in this book provides some support for the public's concern about the potential impact of the current economic crisis on older workers. Specifically, we find evidence that a bear stock market is associated with delayed retirement, but only for more-skilled workers. Although the market has recovered somewhat from its steep decline in 2008–09, it still appears likely that workers now approaching retirement age will experience poor long-term market returns and that some will delay retirement as a result. On the other hand, the notion that falling house prices will have an impact on retirement behavior appears to have little merit.

A more important finding, however, is that the greater impact of the current economic crisis on older workers results from the weak labor market. Less-skilled older workers bear the brunt of this aspect of the crisis. With all of the focus on losses in 401(k)s, the public has overlooked those older workers who are likely to suffer the most.

For reasons that we cannot easily explain, virtually no emphasis has been placed on the damaging effect of an unemployment rate that is nearing post–World War II highs. Job losses are extraordinarily high, and older workers have experienced their share of these losses. Some laid-off older workers may feel they have no choice other than to withdraw from the labor force and begin receiving Social Security benefits to make ends meet, a decision that will result in diminished economic resources throughout their retirement years. Because those at the bottom of the economic ladder are more likely to become unemployed, they will experience the greatest effects.

In a deep recession such as the current one, older workers, particularly those with lower skill levels, are more likely to retire when the labor market weakens. The impact on retirement begins precisely at age sixty-two, when Social Security benefits become available. Hence those benefits appear to serve as a lifeline for those who need income support through some other mechanism if not through work. Claiming Social Security benefits early comes at a cost, however: the monthly benefit amount is reduced, leaving workers with lower levels of income for the rest of their lives. Indeed, individuals who face a weak labor market around the traditional age of retirement have lower incomes ten to fifteen years later. Consistent with our hypothesis that workers claim Social Security benefits earlier when the market is weak, we find that Social Security income falls when the unemployment rate is high around the time of retirement.

Furthermore, the problems resulting from high unemployment are of considerably greater consequence to older workers than those resulting from the falling stock market. First, as we show in this chapter, the absolute number of workers who will be forced to retire as a result of the weak job market is greater than the number of workers who will delay retirement as a result of the weak stock market. Second, the workers affected by the labor market are the ones that the public should care about more—those with fewer resources in the first place. Third, the initial cost of job loss for less-skilled older workers is compounded by the fact that they will typically experience lower income for the remainder of their lives as a result of claiming Social Security benefits sooner. Although the public should not ignore those at the upper end of the income distribution who experience some losses in investment income when the stock market declines, it seems appropriate to give more attention to the group that is more vulnerable to economic shocks. The distributional and policy implications of our analysis are the subject of this chapter.

How Many Workers Are Affected?

In estimating the impact of the economic crisis on retirement, we concentrate on the impact of the falling stock market and rising unemployment because we have found little evidence that falling house prices affect the labor market behavior of older workers (see chapter 5).[1] First, we need to know how many workers could possibly be affected. Drawing on data from the 2005–07 American Community Surveys (ACS), we find that at age fifty-five 2.8 million individuals are in the labor force. By age sixty-nine the number is only 400,000 as most have retired (and some have passed away without having retired).[2]

Next, we use our estimates of the age-specific effect of changing market conditions on retirement to predict changes in retirement. We calculate, for example, that a 5 percentage point increase in the unemployment rate will generate a 1.8 percentage point increase in the likelihood of retirement over the course of a year for workers between the ages of sixty-two and sixty-nine (see chapter 6). We use a five-point increase in the unemployment rate because that is roughly the level of increase that has taken place during the current recession. Our tabulations from the ACS data indicate that there are about 1.4 million sixty-two-year-old workers in the labor force in a given year. According to our estimates, about an additional 25,000 (1,400,000 × .018) of these workers will retire. After conducting this exercise at each age between fifty-five and sixty-nine and then totaling the number of additional retirements likely to result from the current economic crisis, we find that 126,000 additional older workers will retire in response to the higher unemployment rate.

1. For more details regarding these simulations, see Coile and Levine (2009).
2. The baby boom comes into play for those between the ages of fifty-five and sixty who were born in the post–World War II era when birth rates spiked. The size of birth cohorts for those born before this period was similar.

Note, however, that this estimate is the one-year impact of a high unemployment rate. Suppose that it will take five years for the unemployment rate to return to its previous level, falling by one point a year over this period. With the additional retirements from the start of the weak labor market until it returns to normal, about 378,000 additional older workers will end up withdrawing from the labor force as a result of the economic crisis.

For the falling stock market, we start with the same estimates of the number of workers in the labor force at each age. When we assess the impact of long-term changes (say, over ten years) in stock market returns on the likelihood of retiring in a given year (see chapter 4), we find that a 100 percentage point drop in the ten-year return, for example, would reduce the annual likelihood of retirement by 0.63 percentage points for those between the ages of sixty-two and sixty-nine.

If returns dropped 110 percentage points—which would be equivalent to moving from the average ten-year return during the past thirty years (62 percent) to the ten-year return experienced in the period ending in 2008 (–48 percent)[3]—retirement rates would be reduced by 0.69 percentage points for those in this age group. For the 1.4 million workers who are age sixty-two, this means that roughly 10,000 will delay their retirement over the course of a year in response to falling stock prices. When we conduct this exercise at each age and total the age-specific counts, about 86,000 workers annually will delay their retirement because of the stock market crash. Over a five-year period, assuming a steady and gradual return to normal conditions, 258,000 workers will delay their retirement in this case. This value is roughly two-thirds of the number of workers who will be forced to retire early in response to the weakness in the labor market.

Of course, the estimated effect of the recession would not be uniform across the country, owing to marked geographic differences in labor markets. In Michigan, for example, the unemployment rate rose from

3. The stock market has rebounded somewhat since its value at the end of 2008, but we would prefer to take a more conservative approach and err on the side of simulating what may be too large a decline.

6.6 percent in October 2007 to 14.9 percent in March 2010, an increase of 8.3 points. In North Dakota, by contrast, the unemployment rate rose by only 3.0 points, from 2.3 percent in October 2007 to a peak of 5.3 percent in March 2009. These simple statistics suggest that older workers in Michigan would be nearly three times as likely to retire early as a result of the weak labor market as those in North Dakota.

Which Workers Are Affected?

As our calculations suggest, the net effect of the current economic crisis will be to increase retirements, as a greater number of workers will retire early because of the weak labor market than will delay retirement because of the weak stock market. Furthermore, those affected by labor market conditions will tend to have less education and lower levels of income, whereas those affected by the bear market will be individuals near the top of the income distribution.

This finding emerges from our analyses of both retirement decisions and economic well-being in retirement. For practical reasons, we focused on level of education when we examined workers' retirement decisions and level of income when we examined workers' well-being in retirement. Nevertheless, the results in both cases are consistent with our main point.

Our findings with respect to the stock market are not that surprising given that simple descriptive statistics strongly suggest that highly educated or high-income workers should be the main group affected by stock market fluctuations. College-educated workers appear to be the only group with large stockholdings (chapter 4). Even among those who started but did not finish college, the median worker has virtually no stock holdings. Only retirees in the top third of the income distribution receive more than 10 percent of their income in the form of investment income, on average (chapter 3). How can a declining stock market influence the retirement decision or reduce the economic well-being of older workers who have few or no stock assets? Indeed, our more sophisticated empirical analysis confirms our intuition that stock markets should not matter for most workers; we find falling stock prices have no effect on workers outside the highest education and income groups.

Our results do not rule out the possibility that stock market fluctuations could affect a larger share of older workers and retirees in the future. As private pensions continue to shift toward 401(k)-type plans and workers are enrolled in them for a larger share of their working life, the importance of stocks in workers' retirement income will likely grow. Nevertheless, plans of this type are not that common or well funded among workers in their mid-fifties (Gustman and Steinmeier, 2009). It could be twenty or more years before these accounts are sufficiently large and pervasive for stock market fluctuations to play an important role in the well-being of a broader group of retirees. For now, such fluctuations affect primarily the more affluent members of the older population.

Simple statistics also indicate that less-skilled older workers and retirees are more likely to be affected by a weak labor market (chapter 6), for when the labor market contracts, less-skilled workers bear the brunt of the job loss. The employment of more-skilled older workers is the least cyclically responsive. To the extent that labor market difficulties are driving some older workers to retire involuntarily, it seems probable that less-skilled workers will make up a disproportionate share of those in this position.

The cost of job loss may also be greatest for less-skilled workers as those who are laid off and unable to find new work may claim Social Security benefits earlier than they otherwise would. Although total benefits received over an individual's lifetime would not change as a result, the monthly benefit would be lower. Social Security benefits constitute the lion's share of income for lower-income retirees, but only a relatively small share of income for higher-income retirees. Thus early claiming matters more for those at lower income levels.

Formal statistical analysis indicates that labor market fluctuations do matter more for lower-income workers. Lower- and middle-income Social Security recipients experience sizable income losses when the unemployment rate is high around the time that they hit retirement age.

Upper-income retirees are largely unaffected by labor market conditions around the time of their retirement.

Policy Implications

Thus far we have sought to answer a number of questions that fall under the umbrella of positive economics, which is concerned with the description and explanation of economic phenomena ("What is"). By contrast, normative economics draws on both factual information and value judgments to assess the desirability of one course of action as opposed to another ("What should be"). In general, economists are much better at addressing questions of positive economics, which generate objective findings rather than subjective beliefs. Along these lines, we arrived at the following conclusions:

—Long-term declines in stock prices lead older workers to delay retirement.

—High unemployment leads older workers to retire earlier.

—Falling home prices have little impact on older workers' retirement decisions.

—In the current economic crisis, more workers will retire early because of high unemployment than will delay retirement because of declining in stock prices.

—Declining stock prices primarily affect retirement and retiree well-being for more-skilled, upper-income individuals.

—High unemployment primarily affects retirement and retiree well-being for less-skilled, lower-income individuals.

The obvious follow-up question is where do we go from here? At this point, we cross over into the sphere of normative economics, where subjective judgments enter into any policy recommendation, and consensus is not easy to achieve. At the same time, our recommendations clearly rely on the results of positive analysis and target the specific problems identified earlier in the book.

One fairly uncontroversial premise is that losses experienced by the less fortunate are of greater public concern than those felt by the more fortunate. In our context, this means aspects of the current economic crisis that reduce the well-being of the former merit greater attention. It is clear that the weak labor market is the element of the crisis doing the most damage to lower-skilled, lower-income older individuals. Ignoring class distinctions, we estimate that the number of workers adversely affected by the current weak labor market is greater than the number affected by the weak stock market. But even if this were not the case, the fact that those at the bottom of the income distribution are suffering because of the weak labor market might persuade us to focus more on the labor market than the stock market.

Yet public discussion has focused on the effects of the stock market crash and has failed to recognize that most of the workers who are affected by stock losses come from the upper tail of the income distribution. Similarly, falling house prices have received considerable attention although they have had little impact on workers' retirement decisions. The most pressing problem older workers currently face is the labor market, which has received little attention.

Potential Labor Market Policies

In our view, then, the first policy question to address is what can be done to alleviate the labor market difficulty faced by the elderly. Policymakers regularly propose labor market reforms to help disadvantaged workers find jobs and improve their income security, but the policies seldom target older workers. A typical suggestion aimed at the plight of disadvantaged workers is that they be provided with job training. The idea is that if workers have insufficient skills to meet the needs of the modern marketplace, their labor market outcomes may be improved through training in marketable skills. In fact, the federal government funds many job-training programs. The Employment and Training Administration in the U.S. Department of Labor operates many of them, including programs that help adults, youth, dislocated workers, individuals encountering the criminal justice system, migrants and farm workers, and other groups. These programs cost more than $11 billion in fiscal 2010. A natural extension of this system would include older, less-skilled job losers among the targeted groups.

This option is unlikely to have much impact, however. To judge by LaLonde and Sullivan's (2010) review of the research, the evidence supporting the effectiveness of job-training programs is rather thin. Although they focused on youth-training programs—concluding that most such efforts are ineffective at raising skill levels of participants enough to substantially raise their earnings—we believe training programs targeted at older workers are even less likely to be successful. With such a short period of time to recoup investments in training, there would be little incentive for older workers to participate in these types of programs in the first place.

Job search assistance is another standard policy prescription, its programs taking two forms. Some rely on additional checks to verify that unemployed workers, particularly those receiving unemployment insurance benefits, are fulfilling their job search obligations. Others offer job seekers additional services such as assistance in identifying available jobs and writing a résumé. In investigating these programs, Borland and Tseng (2007, p. 358) find that "participation in job search programs appears to improve labor market outcomes for unemployed persons."

The question, then, is to what the extent these programs would be similarly successful for less-skilled older workers who lost their jobs during a recession. On the one hand, older workers might be good candidates for programs assisting with job search, since they are likely to have had longer tenure on their previous job and thus may be behind the times in their knowledge of the job market. Advice regarding where and how to look for work could be particularly beneficial for this group. On the other hand, the fact that these workers lost their jobs as a result of a downturn in the business cycle means that job vacancies are scarce, in which case no amount of search assistance can help older job seekers. Despite evidence that they may be helpful, such programs are unlikely to succeed in a weak labor market or be able to address the problems raised here.

Policymakers also look to wage subsidies as a potential solution to employment problems. The subsidies are generally offered through the tax system, either to the worker or to the firm. The Earned Income Tax Credit is the best-known subsidy directed at workers. Many more subsidy programs have been directed at employers, who typically receive tax breaks if they hire disadvantaged workers.

A wage subsidy might be considered for employers that hire older workers who have lost their jobs during a recession. After reviewing the evidence on the effectiveness of wage subsidy policies more broadly, Neumark (2009) finds they have two significant problems. First, they may deter employers, who may interpret a worker's eligibility for the subsidy as an indication that he or she is unqualified. Second, it is difficult to determine whether these programs actually help create new jobs or simply subsidize firms for hiring workers they would have hired even in the absence of the program. If the latter, then a subsidy targeted at older workers may merely mean an older worker is hired instead of a younger worker, something that is not obviously a desirable outcome. Taken as a whole, wage subsidies do not seem a viable approach to addressing the problems of older workers who lose their job during a recession.

The policies described so far are standard labor market prescriptions that could address the problems of any disadvantaged group of workers. But they are not typically designed to help the aged. Two further ideas are directed specifically at older workers. The first one revolves around preventing age discrimination, which older workers who lose their jobs may face in the hiring process. In fact, before the enactment of the Age Discrimination in Employment Act (ADEA) in 1967, want ads often included an upper bound for the age of applicants. While extreme practices like this were eliminated with the passage of the ADEA, older workers still may be subject to less overt forms of discrimination. If so, tougher enforcement of these laws could help older workers find new jobs when they lose their old ones.

Although this policy has the potential to improve employment outcomes for older workers, it has some limitations. First, in the middle of a recession there is little new hiring of workers of any age, so stricter enforcement of antidiscrimination laws may have little effect. Moreover, ADEA benefits appear to have been concentrated in extending the length of ongoing employment relationships rather than in enhancing the job prospects of older job seekers (Neumark, 2008). Hence this policy may not provide much help to older job losers struggling to find new work.

Yet another policy option builds upon the structure of the unemployment insurance (UI) system. An important empirical finding discussed earlier in our analysis is that laid-off workers appear to stay in the labor market until they reach sixty-two, the age at which they can first claim Social Security benefits. This suggests that workers who are laid off a few years before that age may struggle to find adequate sources of income support until they hit Social Security eligibility. These workers are, in essence, crawling across the finish line.

One model that may be useful in devising ways to help such workers is the disability insurance (DI) program. Its purpose is to provide a bridge to regular Social Security benefits for workers who are unable to work because of health problems. The idea behind the program is that those in poor health are unable to work through no fault of their own. The same could be said of older workers who lose their job in the middle of a major economic downturn. Their inability to find work may say nothing about their desire to work but may simply reflect a drop in demand for their services. Providing displaced older workers with financial assistance (beyond that available through traditional unemployment insurance) is no different from assisting those in poor health.

The chief concern in implementing such a program (for either unemployed or disabled workers), however, is that unemployed workers may adjust their behavior so as to make it more likely they will receive benefits, a phenomenon known as "moral hazard." That is to say, they may curtail their job search efforts if they know government benefits are available to provide income support when they are not working. This is why such a program would only make sense in the context of a major economic downturn, when workers' inability to find a job would presumably have more to do with market realities than with any unwillingness to work.

Interestingly, the DI program may already be serving as a safety net for displaced older workers, at least to some extent. Black, Daniel, and Sanders (2002) and Autor and Duggan (2003) find that DI applications depend on the strength of the labor market. This is unlikely due to cyclical changes in health status that would prevent individuals from working.[4] Rather, it seems more likely that individuals who cannot find jobs are using the DI system as a longer-term form of unemployment insurance. It makes less sense to hide the additional government expenditures in an existing program than to specifically identify the purpose of the expenditure and monitor it accordingly. Moreover, workers' ability to make use of the DI program in this way may depend primarily on their degree of knowledge about the program, rather than their degree of need.

Specifically, we suggest that extended unemployment insurance benefits be offered to workers who lose their jobs at or after age fifty-eight, with a maximum duration dictated by their age rather than by number of weeks of benefits. These benefits would expire precisely at age sixty-two, when the worker would be eligible to claim Social Security retirement benefits. This special benefit extension for older workers would be available only during a recession; it could be triggered in the same way that regular benefit extensions already are. Such a program would likely cost very little, since benefit extensions for workers of all ages already exist—our proposal would merely make benefits available for a longer period of time (up until age sixty-two) for those workers closest to retirement.

Potential Social Security Reforms

Although labor market reforms are the obvious first place to look for possible solutions to the labor market problems of older workers, it makes sense to consider Social Security as well, because of its importance as a source of retirement income. A majority of households aged sixty-five and older receive half or more of their income from Social Security (Social Security Administration, 2010). As we show in chap-

---

4. In fact, Ruhm (2000) argues that workers' health improves during recessions.

ter 7, a worker in the lower third of the income distribution who experiences job loss as retirement is approaching may receive 30 percent less in retirement income, almost entirely because of lower Social Security benefits.

Reforms to Social Security are frequently discussed as a potential means of improving the system's finances or bettering the program in some other way. Their possible effect on unemployed older workers, be it positive or negative, merits some consideration. One such reform, already instituted in 1983, is raising the normal retirement age slowly over time from age sixty-five (for those reaching age sixty-two before 2000) to age sixty-seven (for those reaching age sixty-two in 2022 or later). Some favor accelerating this rise or even increasing the normal retirement age further, perhaps by indexing it to life expectancy so that future increases would be automatic.[5]

As the normal retirement age increases, the penalty for claiming early will increase as well. With normal retirement at age sixty-five, workers claiming at age sixty-two experience a 20 percent reduction in their benefits, but this will rise to 30 percent when normal retirement reaches age sixty-seven. The purpose of this reduction is to ensure that the stream of benefits a worker receives over his or her lifetime is roughly the same regardless of when the worker begins receiving benefits; the earlier a worker claims before the normal retirement age, the larger the benefit reduction. An increase in the normal retirement age may be beneficial for Social Security's finances and may also motivate people to work longer. However, older job losers who are struggling to find new work may feel they have little choice but to claim Social Security benefits when they are first available at age sixty-two, regardless of the impact on their monthly benefit. As a result, further increases in the normal retirement age will only worsen these workers' financial security in retirement.

5. Indexing of the normal retirement age, early entitlement age, and benefit level has already occurred in Denmark, Finland, France, Germany, Japan, Norway, Poland, Portugal, Sweden, and the United Kingdom (AARP Public Policy Institute, 2009).

A related proposal would increase the age at which workers are first eligible for benefits, perhaps in tandem with an increase in the normal retirement age, to reflect the fact that workers are living longer and so should be working longer and claiming retirement benefits later. In some sense, this change would be even more difficult for older job losers struggling to find new work. While raising the normal retirement age would mean a lower monthly benefit amount for those claiming at age sixty-two, raising the early entitlement age would make benefits unavailable at that age, leaving older job losers to endure a longer period of time without income support.

A third proposal suggests increasing the taxation of Social Security benefits.[6] Currently, single taxpayers with incomes in excess of $25,000 a year and married taxpayers with incomes of $32,000 must pay tax on a portion of their benefits. Raising the share of benefits subject to tax or lowering the income limit above which benefits are taxable would increase revenues. The low-income workers who are hurt most by a late-career job loss have such low income that they are not currently affected by the taxation of benefits; however, if all benefits were subject to taxation, low-income workers would be adversely affected.

Since the foregoing reforms seem unlikely to cushion the blow of a late-career layoff and, if anything, could worsen financial security in retirement, one wonders whether other changes could be made to Social Security in order to provide some relief to older job losers. One possible change would be to award older job losers who claim Social Security benefits at age sixty-two (or at any time after that) the same benefit they would have received if they had waited until the normal retirement age to initiate claims. As previously discussed, the current system

6. Among other Social Security reforms that might help to increase older workers' incentive to work, one would be to eliminate the earnings test for workers between the ages of sixty-two and the normal retirement age (a policy that workers tend to view as a tax, though in reality it is not, since workers are credited for any lost benefits by receiving an increased monthly benefit later on); another would be to eliminate the payroll tax on workers once they reach age sixty-two. However, these policies would have little effect on older job losers who are unable to find new work, and so are not discussed in detail here.

incorporates an actuarial adjustment to make lifetime benefits roughly the same regardless of when one retires, which means that the benefits of those claiming at age sixty-two are 20 to 30 percent lower than they would be at the normal retirement age. But if there is a subset of workers for whom job loss precipitates early retirement through no fault of their own, then one policy option would be to provide them with full benefits even if they claim benefits early.

This proposal incorporates the framework of the DI system in much the same way as extending UI benefits until age sixty-two. Indeed, workers on DI face no benefit reduction for claiming Social Security before the normal retirement age, as they are assumed to be unable to continue working and therefore unable to postpone benefit receipt until the normal retirement age. Similarly, older job losers might be considered unable to continue working, so perhaps they too should not have their benefits reduced for early claiming.

A potential problem here, however, is moral hazard. If older job losers knew they could avoid a 20 to 30 percent reduction in their benefit for early claiming by remaining unemployed until age sixty-two, some might not put much effort into looking for a job. Offering an older job loser a lower benefit reduction rather than none would reduce the incentive for this sort of behavior, but it would also provide less assistance to older job losers who were legitimately unable to find a new job. In short, this policy has the potential to be helpful but has important drawbacks as well.

Another option is to alter the Social Security benefit formula in a way that might assist older job losers, rather than change the benefit reduction rate for early retirement. In this vein, one possible tactic would be to give workers some credit in the calculation of their monthly Social Security benefit for the period of time spent in unemployment following a late-career layoff. At present, the monthly benefit is based on a worker's thirty-five best years of earnings, after past earnings have been adjusted by a wage index to bring them up to current levels. Because workers tend to earn higher wages later in their careers, each additional year of work allows many older workers to replace a year with low or zero earnings in the benefit formula. A late-career layoff may prevent the worker from doing this, lowering his or her future Social Security monthly benefit amount.

Therefore we would favor giving workers credit for time spent receiving UI benefits in the calculation of their monthly Social Security amount. Specifically, when older workers are laid off at or after age fifty-eight, their Social Security benefits would be calculated as though they had continued to receive their pre-layoff level of earnings for the period of time during which they were receiving UI benefits. There would be a cost to this policy, since workers would receive an increased Social Security benefit but would not be paying more taxes into the system.

The potential moral hazard in this instance is that workers might ask their employers to lay them off earlier, knowing their Social Security benefits would not be affected. This would undoubtedly be less of an issue here than with some of the other policies just discussed. First, workers may not understand the Social Security benefit formula sufficiently well to recognize the value of receiving this credit during a period in which UI is being received. Second, the immediate impact of the income lost upon layoff may counter the long-term benefit of more generous Social Security benefits, lessening workers' willingness to make this deal with their employers. Third, the benefit of this strategy is small enough in magnitude that it may not provide much of a temptation. All in all, this proposal has the potential to modestly improve the long-term well-being of older workers who experience job loss.

An even simpler solution would be to better communicate one aspect of Social Security rules. Many workers may not be aware that once initiated, the receipt of benefits need not be permanent. A worker is able to stop receiving benefits and then resume them again at a later date.

How does this help? Consider an older worker without a job. Unemployment insurance may help provide income support, but only for a time. Once it runs out, an individual with no other source of income may feel he or she has no choice other than to file a claim for Social Security and begin receiving retirement benefits now, earlier than anticipated. Remember that from the perspective of long-term financial security, the earlier the worker claims, the lower the monthly benefit amount will be. Such workers will have a lower income for the rest of their lives, compared with what they could have had if they had claimed later.

Yet collecting continuously for the remainder of one's life is not a program requirement—a worker can stop receiving benefits at any time. Suppose a worker had planned to retire at age sixty-six but lost his or her job and chose to claim benefits at age sixty-two instead. This individual could continue to look for work and might even locate a new job at age sixty-three, after the labor market had gained some strength. If this worker then chose to stop receiving the benefit and to work until age sixty-seven, and at that point to recommence benefits, from that time on they would be comparable to what he or she would have received without the unemployment spell.[7]

The ability to stop and start benefits is a little-known provision of the program that could be quite valuable to older workers. In essence, this strategy creates a self-funded unemployment insurance system for them.

---

7. For some workers, the Social Security earnings test may function in much the same way as the strategy we have proposed, except that it is not optional. Some further explanation is needed to clarify how it compares with what we propose. Briefly, workers between the ages of sixty-two and the normal retirement age (currently sixty-six—the earnings test does not apply past the normal retirement age) can only earn up to a certain amount ($14,160 in 2010) before the test applies. For any earnings beyond that amount, benefits are reduced by $1 for every $2 in earnings; however, the worker is given credit for benefits lost through the test (for example, if the worker loses $1,000 in benefits and his or her benefit is $1,000 a month, this is treated as having claimed one month later) and the benefit is recomputed accordingly when one reaches the normal retirement age. This part sounds similar to our proposal. A small difference between the earnings test and our proposal is that we suggest the worker stop receiving benefits entirely, whereas the earnings test only reduces benefits beyond a certain level of earnings; our approach would result in a larger readjustment in the benefit later on. A more important difference stems from the fact that many workers seem to treat the earnings test as a tax and are ignorant of the later recomputation of benefits. This has been shown to lead some workers to limit their earnings to levels just below the cutoff (Friedberg, 2000) and may discourage others from even looking for work. So despite the existence of the earnings test, the strategy we propose is a potentially valuable option for workers, and one they should be made more aware of.

They would be able to receive "unemployment" benefits through the Social Security system during their period of greatest need. And because the insurance is self-funded, implementing this strategy would have no budgetary implications for the Social Security Administration, beyond the costs of publicizing it.

Final Thoughts

To reiterate, the public needs to pay more attention to the labor market problems of older workers, particularly those who are less skilled. In our review of labor market policies and Social Security reforms, we find several proposals that we can support. We conclude, first, that it makes sense to extend UI benefits for certain older job losers to age sixty-two during a recession. We define this group as workers who lose their job at or after age fifty-eight. This reform would help older workers bridge the gap between their layoff and the first availability of Social Security benefits. While moral hazard is always a potential concern, it is less likely to be a problem during a recession, when all workers (and perhaps older workers in particular) will face difficulties finding work.

Second, in the calculation of Social Security benefits, older workers who experience a late-career layoff could be credited with the wage from their last job for any period of time spent on unemployment insurance. Substituting the pre-layoff wage for zeroes or years with low earnings in the benefit formula will provide a modest boost to workers' Social Security benefit and thereby improve their financial well-being throughout the rest of their lives.

Third, workers should be informed of the option to stop and start their Social Security benefits. This would encourage laid-off older workers to keep looking for work even once they reach age sixty-two and would reduce the financial consequences of a late-career layoff for those who ultimately found work. Unlike the first two policies, this tactic would impose virtually no cost and no risk of moral hazard.

As noted earlier, answers to normative questions are much more subjective than answers to positive ones. There may be other strategies besides the ones we have discussed to address the problems of older workers approaching retirement when the labor market is weak. Rational discourse on the strengths and weaknesses of whatever alternatives are placed on the table is always a healthy exercise. Regardless of which proposals may ultimately seem most attractive, we stand strongly behind our assertion, based on the results of the analysis we have reported in this book, that more attention needs to be paid to the difficulties faced by individuals who approach retirement at a time when the labor market is weak.

Appendix

Appendix. *Research on the Effect of the Stock Market, Housing Market, and Labor Market on Retirement*

Authors	Data	Methods	Findings
Stock market			
Cheng and French (2000)	PSID	Estimate dynamic structural model of retirement and simulate effect of boom of late 1990s.	Labor force participation rates would have been higher without boom (1.3 points for men 65+, 3.2 points for men 55–64).
Sevak (2001)	HRS	1. Regress retirement on projected unexpected capital gains experienced between 1992 and 1998. 2. Difference-in-difference comparing changes in retirement between 1992 and 1998 for workers with defined contribution pension plans (treatment) to changes for workers with defined benefit plans (control).	1. Regression: doubling retirement consumption increases retirement by 7–9 percentage points. 2. Difference-in-difference: unexpected gain of $50,000 raises retirement by 1.9 percentage points.
Gustman and Steinmeier (2002)	HRS	Estimate structural dynamic model of retirement and saving and simulate effect of boom of late 1990s.	Boom would have decreased average retirement age by about 3 months if it had not been followed by bust.
Coronado and Perozek (2003)	HRS	Regress retirement date on unanticipated stock market gains, controlling for expected retirement date, 1992–2000 data.	Stockholders retire 6 months earlier than expected, compared with non-stockholders; each $100,000 of unanticipated gains leads worker to retire 2 weeks earlier.

Kezdi and Sevak (2004)	CPS, HRS	1. Regress labor force participation on dummy for dividend income interacted with year, 1988–2002 CPS data. 2. Difference-in-difference comparing changes in retirement between 1998 and 2002 for workers with and without stocks, HRS data.	1. From regression: individuals with dividend income are less likely to be in labor force during both boom and bust. 2. From difference-in-difference: no significant differences between two groups.
Coile and Levine (2006)	CPS, HRS	1. Regress retirement on "boom" and "bust" dummies by demographic group (stock ownership proxy), 1980–2002 data. 2. Same but use change in S&P 500 Index over past 12 months.	1. No evidence that retirement rises in boom and falls in bust for groups more exposed to market fluctuations compared with others. 2. No evidence of differential response to returns by stock proxy group.
Coile and Levine (2009)	CPS	Regress retirement on change in S&P 500 Index over past 1, 5, and 10 years by demographic group (stock ownership proxy), 1980–2006 data.	Workers 62–69 with more education respond to 5- and 10-year stock returns (retire earlier if get a larger positive return); younger workers and less-educated workers do not respond.
Hurd, Reti, and Rohwedder (2009)	HRS	Regress changes between survey waves (2-year period) in subjective probability of working past age 62 on stockholder status, 1992–2002 data.	No evidence that workers with larger gains revise retirement expectations compared with workers without gains.
Housing market			
Coile and Levine (2009)	CPS	Regress retirement on fluctuations in local or state housing index, by homeowner status, 1980–2006 data.	No evidence that house price movements affect retirement decisions of homeowners compared with renters.

(continued)

Appendix. *Research on the Effect of the Stock Market, Housing Market, and Labor Market on Retirement* (*Continued*)

Authors	Data	Methods	Findings
Labor market			
Coile and Levine (2007)	CPS	Regress retirement rate on unemployment rate, 1980–2004 data. Also explore whether generosity of unemployment insurance (UI) matters.	Retirement increases with the unemployment rate, starting at age 61. Effect is concentrated in transitions with a spell of unemployment and/or UI receipt. More generous UI benefits do not decrease retirement.
von Wachter (2007)	CPS, DWS	Regress employment by industry, state, and year on changes in industry-level employment and state unemployment rate.	Industry-level employment and state unemployment rates affect labor force participation of older workers.
Hallberg (2008)	Swedish microdata	Regress retirement on industry-specific deviations in employment from long-run trends.	Retirement increases when there are short-term decreases in aggregate employment.
Coile and Levine (2009)	CPS	Regress retirement on unemployment rate, 1980–2006 data.	Retirement increases with the unemployment rate; response is concentrated among older workers (62–69) and those with less education.

PSID = Panel Study of Income Dynamics; CPS = Current Population Survey; HRS = Health and Retirement Study; DWS = Displaced Worker Survey.

References

AARP Public Policy Institute. 2009. "Social Security Financing: Automatic Adjustments to Restore Solvency." Brief 166. Washington.

Alexander, J. Trent, Michael Davern, and Betsey Stevenson. 2010. "Inaccurate Age and Sex Data in the Census PUMS Files: Evidence and Implications." Working Paper 15703. Cambridge, Mass.: National Bureau of Economic Research.

Anderson, Kathryn H., and Richard V. Burkhauser. 1985. "The Retirement-Health Nexus." *Journal of Human Resources* 20, no. 3: 315–30.

Arias, Elizabeth. 2007. "United States Life Tables, 2004." *National Vital Statistics Reports* 56, no. 9: 1–40.

Autor, David H., and Mark G. Duggan. 2003. "The Rise in the Disability Rolls and the Decline in Unemployment." *Quarterly Journal of Economics* 118, no. 1: 157–205.

Bazzoli, Gloria. 1985. "The Early Retirement Decision." *Journal of Human Resources* 20, no. 2: 214–34.

Black, Dan, Kermit Daniel, and Seth Sanders. 2002. "The Impact of Economic Conditions on Participation in Disability Programs: Evidence from the Coal Boom and Bust." *American Economic Review* 92, no. 1: 27–50.

Black, Dan A., and Xiaoli Liang. 2005. "Local Labor Market Conditions and Retirement Behavio." Working Paper 2005-08. Boston College Center for Retirement Research.

Blau, David M., and Donna B. Gilleskie. 2001. "Retiree Health Insurance and the Labor Force Behavior of Older Men in the 1990s." *Review of Economics and Statistics* 83, no. 1: 64–80.

Borland, Jeff, and Yi-Ping Tseng. 2007. "Does a Minimum Job Search Requirement Reduce Time on Unemployment Payments? Evidence from the Jobseeker Diary in Australia." *Industrial and Labor Relations Review* 60, no. 3: 357–78.

Bruce, Donald, Douglas Holtz-Eakin, and Joseph Quinn. 2000. "Self-Employment and Labor Market Transitions at Older Ages." Working Paper 2000-13. Boston College Center for Retirement Research.

Burtless, Gary, and Robert Moffitt. 1986. "Social Security, Earnings Tests, and Age at Retirement." *Public Finance Quarterly* 14, no. 1: 3–27.

Cahill, Kevin E., Michael D. Giandrea, and Joseph F. Quinn. 2005. "Are Traditional Retirements a Thing of the Past? New Evidence on Retirement Patterns and Bridge Jobs." Working Papers in Economics 626. Boston College.

Chan, Sewin, and Ann Huff Stevens. 1999. "Employment and Retirement Following a Late-Career Job Loss." *American Economic Review* 89, no. 2: 211–16.

Cheng, Ing-Haw, and Eric French. 2000. "The Effect of the Run-Up in the Stock Market on Labor Supply." *Economic Perspectives*, Quarter 4: 48–65.

Coile, Courtney C., and Jonathan Gruber. 2007. "Future Social Security Entitlements and the Retirement Decision." *Review of Economics and Statistics* 89 (May): 234–46.

Coile, Courtney C., and Phillip B. Levine. 2006. "Bulls, Bears, and Retirement Behavior." *Industrial and Labor Relations Review* 59 (April): 408–29.

———. 2007. "Labor Market Shocks and Retirement: Do Government Programs Matter?" *Journal of Public Economics* 91 (November):1902–19.

———. 2009. "The Market Crash and Mass Layoffs: How the Current Economic Crisis May Affect Retirement." Working Paper 15395. Cambridge, Mass.: National Bureau of Economic Research.

———. 2010. "Recessions, Reeling Markets and Retiree Well-Being." Working Paper 16066. Cambridge, Mass.: National Bureau of Economic Research.

Coronado, Julia Lynn, and Maria G. Perozek. 2003. "Wealth Effects and the Consumption of Lesiure: Retirement Decisions during the Stock Market Boom of the 1990s." Finance and Economic Discussion Series 2003-20. Washington: Board of Governors of the Federal Reserve System.

Costa, Dora L. 1998. *The Evolution of Retirement: An American Economic History, 1880–1990.* University of Chicago Press.

Currie, Janet, and Brigitte C. Madrian. 1999. "Health, Health Insurance, and the Labor Market." In *Handbook of Labor Economics,* vol. 3C, edited by Orley Ashenfelter and David Card. New York: Elsevier.

Diamond, Peter, and Jonathan Gruber. 1999. "Social Security and Retirement in the United States." In *Social Security and Retirement around the World,* edited by David A. Wise and Jonathan Gruber. University of Chicago Press.

Employee Benefit Research Institute. 2009. *EBRI Databook on Employee Benefits.* Washington.

Eschtruth, Andrew D., Wei Sun, and Anthony Webb. 2006. "Will Reverse Mortgages Rescue the Baby Boomers?" Issue Brief 54. Boston College Center for Retirement Research.

Farber, Henry S. 2005. "What Do We Know about Job Loss in the United States? New Evidence from the Displaced Worker Survey, 1984–2004." *Economic Perspectives* (Federal Reserve Bank of Chicago) 29, no. 2: 13–28.

———. 2010. "Job Loss and the Decline in Job Security in the United States." In *Labor in the New Economy,* edited by Katharine G. Abraham, James R. Spletzer, and Michael Harper. Chicago: University of Chicago Press.

Feldstein, Martin S., and Jeffrey B. Liebman. 2002. "Social Security." In *Handbook of Public Economics,* vol. 4, edited by Alan J. Auerbach and Martin S. Feldstein. New York: Elsevier.

Friedberg, Leora. 2000. "The Labor Supply Effects of the Social Security Earnings Test." *Review of Economics and Statistics* 82 (February): 48–63.

Friedberg, Leora, and Anthony Webb. 2005. "Retirement and the Evolution of the Pension Structure." *Journal of Human Resources* 40, no. 2: 281–308.

Friedberg, Leora, Michael Owyang, and Anthony Webb. 2008. "Identifying Local Differences in Retirement Patterns." Working Paper 2008-18. Boston College Center for Retirement Research.

Fronstin, Paul. 2007. "The Future of Employment-Based Health Benefits: Have Employers Reached a Tipping Point?" Issue Brief 312. Washington: Employee Benefit Research Institute.

Garr, Emily. 2009. "Older Americans in the Recession: More Are Staying in the Workforce, More Are Losing Their Jobs." Issue Brief 251. Washington: Economic Policy Institute.

GfK Roper Public Affairs & Media. 2008. *The AP-GfK Poll* (interview dates September 27–30, 2008). New York: GfK Custom Research.

Goss, Stephen C. 2009. *Applications for Social Security Retired Worker Benefits in Fiscal Year 2009.* Washington: Social Security Administration, Office of the Chief Actuary.

Gruber, Jonathan, and Brigitte Madrian. 1995. "Health Insurance Availability and the Retirement Decision." *American Economic Review* 85, no. 4: 938–48.

Gruber, Jonathan, and David A. Wise. 1999. *Social Security and Retirement around the World.* University of Chicago Press.

Gustman, Alan L., and Thomas Steinmeier. 2002. "Retirement and the Stock Market Bubble." Working Paper 9404. Cambridge, Mass.: National Bureau of Economic Research.

———. 2008. "How Changes in Social Security Affect Recent Retirement Trends." Working Paper 14105. Cambridge, Mass.: National Bureau of Economic Research.

Gustman, Alan L., Thomas L. Steinmeier, and Nahid Tabatabai. 2009. "What the Stock Market Decline Means for the Financial Security and Retirement Choices of the Near Retirement Population." Working Paper 15435. Cambridge, Mass.: National Bureau of Economic Research.

———. Forthcoming. *Pensions in the Health and Retirement Study. 2010.* Harvard University Press.

Hallberg, Daniel. 2008. "Economic Fluctuations and the Retirement of Elderly Workers." Working Paper Series 2008:5. Institute for Labor Market Policy Evaluation.

Hurd, Michael. 1990. "Research on the Elderly: Economic Status, Retirement, and Consumption and Saving." *Journal of Economic Literature* 28, no. 2: 565–637.

Hurd, Michael, Monika Reti, and Susann Rohwedder. 2009. "The Effect of Large Capital Gains or Losses on Retirement." In *Developments in the Economics of Aging*, edited by David A. Wise. University of Chicago Press.

Jacobson, Louis, Robert LaLonde, and Daniel Sullivan. 1993. "Earnings Losses of Displaced Workers." *American Economic Review* 83, no. 4: 685–709.

Kezdi, Gabor, and Purvi Sevak, 2004. "Economic Adjustment of Recent Retirees to Adverse Wealth Shocks." Working Paper 2004-075. Ann Arbor: Michigan Retirement Research Center.

LaLonde, Robert, and Daniel Sullivan. 2010. "Vocational Training." In *Targeting Investments in Children: Fighting Poverty When Resources Are Limited*, edited by Phillip B. Levine and David J. Zimmerman. University of Chicago Press.

Lambrinos, James. 1981. "Health: A Source of Bias in Labor Supply Models." *Review of Economics and Statistics* 63, no. 2: 206–12.

Levine, Phillip B. 1993. "A Comparison of Contemporaneous and Retrospective Measures of Unemployment from the Current Population Survey." *Monthly Labor Review* 116, no. 8: 33–38.

Lumsdaine, Robin L., and Olivia S. Mitchell, 1999. "Economic Analysis of Retirement." In *Handbook of Labor Economics,* vol. 3C, edited by Orley Ashenfelter and David Card. New York: Elsevier.

Maestas, Nicole. 2007. "Back to Work: Expectations and Realizations of Work after Retirement." Working Paper WR-196-2. Santa Monica, Calif.: RAND.

Martin, Patricia P., and David A. Weaver. 2005. "Social Security: A Program and Policy History." *Social Security Bulletin* 66, no. 1: 1–15.

McGarry, Kathleen, and Robert F. Schoeni. 2005. "Widow(er) Poverty and Out-of-Pocket Medical Expenditures Near the End of Life." *Journals of Gerontology Series B: Psychological Sciences and Social Sciences* 60, no. 3: S160–68.

Munnell, Alicia H., Mauricio Soto, Robert K. Triest, and Natalia A. Zhivan. 2008. "How Much Do State Economics and Other Characteristics Affect Labor Force Participation of Older Workers?" Working Paper 2008-12. Boston College Center for Retirement Research.

Neumark, David. 2008. "The Age Discrimination in Employment Act and the Challenge of Population Aging." Working Paper 14317. Cambridge, Mass.: National Bureau of Economic Research.

————. 2009. "Alternative Labor Market Policies to Increase Economic Self-Sufficiency: Mandating Higher Wages, Subsidizing Employment, and Increasing Productivity." Working Paper 14807. Cambridge, Mass: National Bureau of Economic Research.

Ruggles, Steven, and others. 2009. *Integrated Public Use Microdata Series: Version 4.0* [Machine-readable database]. Minneapolis: Minnesota Population Center.

Ruhm, Christopher. 2000. "Are Recessions Good for Your Health?" *Quarterly Journal of Economics* 115, no. 2: 617–50.

Sammartino, Frank. 1987. "The Effect of Health on Retirement." *Social Security Bulletin* 50, no. 2: 31–47.

Sevak, Purvi. 2001. "Wealth Shocks and Retirement Timing: Evidence from the Nineties." Working Paper 2002-027. Michigan Retirement Research Center.

Social Security Administration. 2008. *Annual Statistical Supplement to the Social Security Bulletin, 2008.* SSA Publication 13-11700. Washington.

————. 2010. *Income of the Aged Chartbook, 2008.* SSA Publication 13-11727. Washington.

Stock, James, and David Wise. 1990. "Pensions, the Option Value of Work, and Retirement." *Econometrica* 58, no. 5: 1151–80.

Taylor, Paul, and others. 2009. *America's Changing Workforce Recession Turns a Graying Office Grayer.* Washington: Pew Research Center.

Venti, Steven F., and David A. Wise. 2004. "Aging and Housing Equity: Another Look." In *Perspectives on the Economics of Aging,* edited by David A. Wise. University of Chicago Press.

Ventura, Stephanie J., and others. 2009. "Estimated Pregnancy Rates for the United States, 1990–2005: An Update." *National Vital Statistics Reports* 58, no. 4.

von Wachter, Till M. 2007. "The Effect of Economic Conditions on the Employment of Workers Nearing Retirement Age." Working Paper 2007-025. Boston College Center for Retirement Research.

von Wachter, Till M., Jae Song, and Joyce Manchester. 2008. "Long-Term Earnings Losses due to Mass Layoffs during the 1982 Recession: An Analysis Using U.S. Administrative Data from 1974 to 2004." Unpublished manuscript. Columbia University.

Index